The Stroke of a Pen

The Stroke of a Pen

ESSAYS ON POETRY AND OTHER PROVOCATIONS

SAMUEL HAZO

University of Notre Dame Press

Notre Dame, Indiana

Manufactured in the United States of America

Library of Congress Cataloging-in-Publication Data

Hazo, Samuel John.
The stroke of a pen : essays on poetry and other provocations / Samuel Hazo.
p.   cm.
Includes bibliographical references.
ISBN-13: 978-0-268-03094-0 (pbk. : alk. paper)
ISBN-10: 0-268-03094-4 (pbk. : alk. paper)
I. Title.
PS3515.A9877S77   2011
814'.54—dc22

2010052721

In Memoriam

Albert C. Labriola

Scholar, Teacher, Colleague, Friend

CONTENTS

PREFACE

Everything I've ever written I've initially written by hand. Poetry, fiction, essays, plays—they all began when the nib of my fountain pen touched paper. Later would come the final drafts on a typewriter or eventually on a word processor or computer. But it all started with a pen in my right hand. A fountain pen. Writing with a ballpoint or a pencil seemed somehow both unacceptable and unauthentic, as if I were signing a bad check.

In the essays in this book on poetry, power, music, knowledge, faith, literary criticism, travel, home, friendship, and what is erroneously called retirement (a term I hate because it is both inaccurate and to me demeaning), I found that writing with a pen matched the pace of my thought as it evolved. That's the reason why being a penman has always defined for me what it means to be a writer. I have written each essay in this book like a letter to a close friend. Nothing but expressing the whole truth has been my criterion, as it should be between friends. I hope the reader will find himself addressed in this spirit from the first page to the last.

Grateful acknowledgment goes to *Sewanee Review, Renascence, Notre Dame Magazine, University of Pittsburgh American Experience Program, Vital Speeches,* and *Carnegie Magazine,* in which some of these essays first appeared. I would also like to thank William O'Rourke for suggesting the apt subtitle of this book.

I

Poetry and Public Speech

Most people would concede that what is truly important is what we cannot forget even if we try. This could be events, persons, places, or words spoken or written. Unlike words, most events, persons, and places tend to live on like aging photographs. We see them within the parentheses of their years, months, and days. Often to our regret they have dated lives. But memorable words seem to have an undying legacy, and they survive the times and places of their origin without difficulty. How? Perhaps it is because they retain their original energy and express something that is permanently true. It is inherent in how Sophocles has Haimon answer his father Creon in *Antigone* after Haimon had been reprimanded for having the temerity to correct his elders: "But if I am young and right, what difference does it make if I am young?" Or it could be Saint Paul's "Yea, though I speak with the tongues of men and of angels and have not charity, I am become as sounding brass or a tinkling cymbal." Why have these words kept their original life? What makes them unforgettable?

In a letter to the philosopher Sidney Cox, Robert Frost stresses that an essential difference exists between a grammatically correct sentence and a living sentence. He does not define the difference, but he suggests that a living sentence could be identified by its undismissable effect. I would suggest that these lines from Frost's "The Death of the Hired Man" would qualify as a living sentence: "Home is the place where, when you have to go there, / They have to take you in." And the same sense of life is present in the four sentences that constitute an early poem of Frost's entitled "November":

We saw leaves go to glory,
Then almost migratory
Go part way down the lane,
And then to end the story
Get beaten down and pasted
in a wild day of rain.

We heard " 'Tis over" roaring.
A year of leaves was wasted.
Oh, we make a boast of storing,
Of saving and of keeping,
But only by ignoring
The waste of moments sleeping,
The waste of pleasure weeping,
By denying and ignoring
The waste of nations warring.

These lines live because they succeed in expressing felt thought in its fullness and let us share the feeling as we absorb the thought. We listen with our whole selves, not merely from the eyebrows up. All the words contribute to a unified poetic effect and persuade us that the expression is as perfect as possible for its purpose. It meets Henry David Thoreau's standard: "What is once well done is done forever." It creates the power of the imperishable example. Its memorability follows from this. The words last as written or said because the inimitable has no substitutes. It lets itself be known by heart, which is the best form of knowledge because it confirms it as an ongoing presence. And ongoing presences have no past tense.

The difference between the transitory and the permanent is obvious if we compare living or poetic lines with the following journalistic examples. "The idea of canning a huge, flavorful beer was anathema in the bottle-fetish craft-brewing world where cans were associated with mass-produced plonk." Or "Clint Eastwood takes an intimate look at the public face of war." Both sentences are grammatically correct, but all that they convey is information, as intended. They exist, but they do not live. They do not have the quality that is identified in Spanish as *sentipensante,* feeling/thinking. Anyone could have written them, even a committee. In either case they lack the staying power of Frost's lines because the lines of his poem are not mere statements but utterances; the spiritual impetus and energy of their author are behind them and in them.

I do not make this comparison to denigrate the language of statement, which does serve a necessary purpose. Regardless, it is not language at its fullest. Once it has served its purpose, it evaporates. But this is the language that dominates our public life. It is expository prose in varying degrees of directness and style—almost all of it eventually forgettable. Social scientists have estimated that each of us is bombarded daily by thousands of similar forms of expression, either seen or heard. Of the thousands that we may have heard as recently as yesterday, are there any that resist being forgotten? Is there one? Think of the language of advertising, which is language designed to persuade, seduce, or otherwise induce compliance that will result in sales. How much of it sticks, even if we succumb? And what of the language of government, which inclines toward, more often than we like to admit, propaganda? The journalist I. F. Stone, who has been deservedly praised for indicting various politicians by using their own words against them, believed as a matter of political fact (and so wrote) that all governments lie—some less skillfully than others, some adroitly, but all shamelessly. Lying in its essence is not merely a trivial fault. It is a perversion of language itself. It does injustice to the social contract. No wonder that Saint Augustine regarded lying as a grave sin, not merely because it corrupted the currency of speech but also because it placed itself in opposition to divine law.

Though lying qualifies as one of the most serious of the perversions of language, there are a slew of lesser offenders, namely, gossip, small talk, low slang, and blasphemy. Of course, there are times in this cornucopia of usage when there are pleasant "poetic surprises," albeit just this side of clever. The phonetically prone *Chicago Tribune* came up with this headline some years ago: STATE HIKES FRATE RATE. Overlook the deliberate misspelling, and you have a fine example of internal rhyme. Headline writers and public relations types have been adopting poetic tropes for years to suit their purposes. Remember the slogan that helped elect Dwight Eisenhower: *I Like Ike!* And automobile pitchmen have never had an aversion to alliteration, as in Lexus's "passionate pursuit of perfection." In some journalism, a genuine poetic impulse manages to transcend what is habitually expected, as in this headline that announced the death of the Italian novelist Alberto Moravia: SENZA MORAVIA (Without Moravia). It may not have been journalistically correct, but it must have captured the pathos of that moment. Using the same headline technique after President Kennedy's assassination on November 22, 1963, would undoubtedly have had a similar effect. Another classical example of a headline that was poetically inspired happened after Manolete, the greatest Spanish matador of the twentieth century, was fatally gored at the very instant that he stabbed his last bull in the last *faena* of the last bullfight of the last tour of his life: MATÓ MURIÉNDOSE, Y SE MURIÓ MATANDO (He killed dying, and he died killing).

Such unexpected poetry happens almost by accident, as if the ordinary diction of our lives finds itself unequal to a challenge. Slang, for example, has been known to identify subjects more imaginatively than the proper nouns by which we know them: "jarhead" instead of Marine, "Sooner" instead of Oklahoman, "jock" instead of "athlete." As for blasphemy there is now no question that the usual four-letter words are overworked clichés. They seem almost childish when compared with this remarkable curse by Robert Desnos: "Cursed / be the father of the bride / of the blacksmith who forged the iron for the axe / with which the woodsman hacked down the oak / from which the bed was carved / in which was conceived the great-grandfather / of the man who was driving the carriage / in which your mother met your father!"

Hayden Carruth once identified poetry as "the voice that is great within us"—within all of us. And he is correct. But why is this voice missing in almost all of our public discourse, except in those instances when it seems beyond suppression? Why shouldn't poetry occupy a central position in our cultural life if it is indeed the apogee of language and literature and offers us, according to T. S. Eliot, "excellent words in excellent arrangement"? After all, a society exists when human beings live not in isolation but in conjunction with one another and where they face individually and collectively all the trials that "flesh is heir to" while simultaneously striving to perfect those capabilities—speech, imagination, reverence for life, to name only a few—that distinguish them from all other creatures. In such circumstances it would seem that experiencing "excellent words in excellent arrangement" would help them to live in harmony while inspiring them to live justly and fully. But as long as people see themselves living not in a society but in an economy, they naturally become more inclined to regard themselves (or to be regarded by others) simply as consumers, purchasers, assets, personnel, litigants, contributors, liabilities, and so on. Their daily vocabularies tend to be filled with words that are in vogue, such as gross national product, downsizing, profit and loss ratios, and personal worth versus marketplace value. By this latter standard a person is measured by his assets. If he has thousands or millions to his name, he is worth thousands or millions. If he has nothing, he is worth nothing. In time this language becomes the language of quantity, not quality—the language of abstraction and generality and not the language of felt thought. It becomes the language of inhumanity.

If the language of an economy becomes the working vocabulary of our lives, then it can leave out many of those elements that sustain us as human beings. Also, in the face of tragedy or reversal or disappointment or betrayal, it is simply out of its depth, and the person so affected is left adrift, searching for answers or acceptances that are not in his dictionary. I wrote a poem some years ago in which I tried to come to terms with such a state by assuming for the length of the poem the character of a man who dealt in financial instruments, as they are called. Instead of espousing the view that we are on this earth to work at what we love as long as we are able to do so, he believed that the desired goal of a diligent life was to be able to ease off into a life of what the poet Richard Wilbur described as "affluent privacy." In other words, you work only so you won't have to work, and that is the only reason you work.

At its best the language of an economy is the language of information. At its worst it is the language of hidden persuasion and of
"spin." All too often it is at the service of a program, an ideology, or,
in a totalitarian state or system, it is the language of dementia and
fear. Its goal is to manipulate, not enlighten; to arouse, not stir; to
deaden, not quicken. The chief difference between poetry and the
language of information in an economy is depressingly obvious.
Where poetry illuminates and addresses itself to our common humanity, the language of an economy speaks to a common denomi-
nator of its own creation, usually, though not always, the lowest. Who,
for example, lives in a statistical family of two-and-a-half children or
considers the deaths of more than 4,000 soldiers in Iraq "minimally
acceptable"? Or what kind of a human being would find it comfort-
ing to know that the aforementioned number of war dead does not
begin to approximate the number of highway deaths per annum in
our own country?

Because poetry is the language of felt thought and utterance (a
poet, said Ezra Pound, is a "man believing in silence [who] found
himself unable to withhold himself from speaking"), of admissions
and oaths as sacred as life itself, it is evident in an economy by its
absence. As long as people are perceived in economic terms alone,
poetry (and all the other arts, for that matter) will be regarded as
ornamental or irrelevant or simply dispensable. If people are more
than mere economic integers, then the disregard of poetry will be as
fatal to their spiritual lives as the deprivation of oxygen would be to
their physical lives. Why? Because poetry tells us who we are, what
our surroundings mean to us, and what waits to be discovered beneath the apparent. In such ways poetry is our means of rendering
justice to the world and to our place in it. It is a language spoken as
necessarily and often as involuntarily as a scream or a laugh or what
the poet George Seferis identified as "the small white cries of love." It
is the language of the heart (by which we know ourselves and which,
in Pascal's words, "has reasons that the reason does not know"). It is
at the same time the language of the senses, through which we know
the world.

To say that poetry is as essential to our spiritual lives as oxygen
is to our physical lives is not a mere figure of speech. The fact is that

human beings cannot deny their need to feel the full range of life's integral emotions any more than they can consider oxygen a mere option. People cannot live unfeelingly, however hard the stoic within them may try. Without meeting or even acknowledging their need for feeling, people are reduced to dullness, which is self-imposed solitary confinement. Such people become disassociated from the wellsprings of personal and social health. An economy, of course, is quite indifferent to that. It wants no more than a population composed of puritans of industry. The entire American capitalist system is rooted in that. But the human spirit is not. It craves the solidarity of feeling. The aforementioned T. S. Eliot not only thought of poetry as "excellent words in excellent arrangement" but was convinced that precise feeling could be expressed only in this way. And feelings, as every human being must eventually admit, move inexorably toward expression. And the expression of exact feeling, as Eliot further stressed, is more difficult than the expression of exact thought.

And who but poets—or any child or adult when moved to say something in a spontaneous and poetic way—fulfill this need in a society? Here are two examples. One is a single sentence reported to me by my son when he was dealing with a group of gifted middle-school students after the class had returned from a tour of a historic house. Referring to the spacious living room there, one boy said, "The room was so big that I felt rich." A second example is by the Spanish poet Antonio Machado. These two lines by Machado are quoted throughout the Spanish-speaking world, and they resonate with all of us when we realize that life's script cannot be foreseen because we ourselves are the script that we are writing from day to day for as long as we live: "Caminante, no hay camino. / Se hace camino al andar." (Wayfarer, there is no road. / You make the road as you go.)

Reading or hearing words like these expressed in this way—experiencing these *felt* thoughts—both confirms and eases some emotion in us. It reassures us that we have the right to feel what we feel simply because we do. We live thereafter quickened and deepened. People to whom poetry is anathema are never stirred in this way. For their emotional life they turn to mere entertainment or risk-taking or gambling or the emotional orgies of football games or political conventions or pornography or the periodic facsimiles of pointless frivolity and noise that we associate with New Year's Eve. This is nothing but indulgence that leaves no echo. At best it's a distraction. At worst it's an escape. It numbs us. It does not reward us with what Robert Frost called "a momentary stay against confusion." Momentary is the pivotal word here. Poems tend to be momentary; they stop us in our emotional tracks. Protracted, such moments would slowly deflate. In a comparable way comedy prolonged becomes comedy diluted and eventually squandered. The prolongation leads to farce or burlesque, and the response of the observers is either derision or embarrassment. Similarly, tragedy that is unrelieved makes what is poignant melodramatic and eventually boring. Even the impulse in all of us to go on living—as if life and longevity are interchangeable—is contradicted by the fact that whole lifetimes can be and often are compressed into a single instant of joy, love, grief, or triumph. Merely *living on* is not synonymous with what it means *to be alive* since protraction only gains in duration what it loses in intensity.

True poems are momentary intensities, and they are invariably as brief as they are unforgettable. They startle us into the ongoing time of the present tense, and they keep us there as long as we are in their grip. Like the times of kisses or tears, they have no past or future tense. Like telegrams they eschew the superfluous and stress the vital. They emphasize the power of less, calling to mind that principle in physics that shows how the more you reduce the spatial volume, the more you increase the pressure. In poetic expression we strive for that succinctness, missing it more often than finding it but striving on. Gustave Flaubert was expressing the same sentiment when he claimed that "human speech is like a cracked kettle on which we tap crude rhythms for bears to dance to, while we long to make music that will melt the stars."

True poetic utterance is born of necessity coupled with reflection, of stepping back and perceiving the passing moment as it is and not as it appears to be. In an economy where reality is often distorted or contorted to support an ulterior worldview or agenda, the goal is often not to say what is true but what will breed compliance and keep the economy going. To such ends, language is often merchandised and cheapened, and what we are usually left with is a lie. Misused in this way, language is corrupted, and this corruption has led to everything from confusion to war, as our own recent history regrettably now confirms. If poetry has no other claim for our attention, then the fact that it has no truck with lies is sufficient justification for its value. And the men or women who are momentarily inspired to make such utterances need no further credential than the truth of what they are enlightened to express, as was the child before the unclothed emperor who simply said what was there — or, as it turned out, not there. "Wise words are rarer than emeralds," runs the ancient Egyptian adage, "yet they come from the mouths of poor slave girls who turn the millstones."

It is a maxim among optometrists that the human eye by its very nature demands a single clear image. It is dissatisfied with anything less, which explains why the correctives of glasses, lenses, eyedrops, or even surgery are at times imperative. Anyone who strives to express the testimony of the heart or the senses is never satisfied if what is said or written is not the equivalent of what is felt or sensed. It is one thing for an athlete to say, "I love sports," but it is something else entirely for him to say, "I love to play basketball more than I like to eat when I'm hungry." And if we proceed from a love of sports to the love of a particular person, who can improve upon John Donne's statement in "The Paradox" to suggest that love has no past tense: "I cannot say I loved, for who can say / He was killed yesterday?" And in the same vein there is this scene in Edmond Rostand's *Cyrano de Bergerac* when Roxane, thinking she loves Christian, is thoroughly disillusioned when he cannot convince her of it from his hidden place beneath her balcony. All Christian can say is, "I love you." When Roxane answers, "We have the theme, / Now play the variations," Christian can only muster, "I love you very much." Eventually, Cyrano, who truly loves Roxane, takes Christian's place in the darkness and begins to speak for him: "I love, I am choked with love, I love, I rave / With love, more love there cannot be, it brims / and overflows, a cataract of dreams. / Your name rings like a sheep-bell in my heart, / I tremble and its sounds — Roxane! No part / Of any day is forgotten if you were there." Roxane, thinking it is Christian who is speaking, falls in love with Cyrano's words, confirming again the truth of the old Arab proverb: "Love comes to men through the eye, to women through the ear."

The marriage of poetry and public life is not, nor has ever been, a forced marriage in human history. The visionary voice of poetry is heard in the words of the Old Testament prophets, in the beatitudes of Christ, in the lines of Sophocles and Virgil, in the ballads of François Villon, in the poems of Padraic Pearse and William Butler Yeats during the Irish Troubles as well as in the poems of Seamus Heaney in our own era, in the work of Paul Eluard and René Char during the French Resistance, in the elegant and defiant poems of Czeslaw Milosz and Wislawa Szymborska in Polish, of Hans Magnus Enzensberger in German, of Adonis in Arabic, of Gabriel Celaya in Spanish, of Tomas Tranströmer in Swedish, of Leonardo Sinisgalli in Italian, of Yannis Ritsos in Greek, and of Carlos Drummond de Andrade in Portuguese. It is the same visionary voice that we hear in the poetry of Robert Frost, Dylan Thomas, Archibald MacLeish, e. e. cummings, Randall Jarrell, Richard Wilbur, Linda Pastan, Naomi Shihab Nye, and numerous others. All of the poems of these men and women fulfill the mission that the Nobel Laureate Saint-John Perse enjoined upon poets everywhere—to be "the guilty conscience of their time." In this way they can make us aware feelingly of what matters and what does not. And in their "craft or art" they confirm that truth will always outlive lies in the same way that love will always outlive death.

T W O

Power and Pretense

It is ironic but true that power in its most obvious forms is the least enduring while power in its least obvious forms is the most enduring. For proof, consider the following. If asked to define the essence of power, most Americans (and indeed most people throughout the world) would equate power with strength. They would say unhesitatingly that they would consider any nation (the United States, Russia, or China, for example) powerful if it possessed formidable military assets. By the same standard they would consider any nation weak whose military strengths were in comparison negligible, such as Lebanon, Denmark, or Switzerland. At present the United States of America is considered the most powerful nation on earth for the simple reason that its military assets are second to none.

But if the capacity to endure is the hallmark of true power (and I believe that it is and must be), then history demonstrates again and again that so-called "powerful nations" frequently had a short lifespan before their power waned or was superseded by a "stronger power." In 1926, Paul Valéry wrote: "In modern times no single power or empire in Europe has been able to stand supreme, to dominate others far and near or even to retain its conquests for longer than fifty years. The greatest men have failed to achieve this object, and even the most fortunate led their countries to ruin: Charles V, Louis XIV, Napoleon, Metternich, Bismarck: average span—fifty years. There are no exceptions." Valéry easily could have added the names of Hitler, Mussolini, and Tojo, and his conclusion would still apply since Hitler's Reich, Mussolini's fascist Italy, and Tojo's militarized Japan lasted for mere decades. And the USSR could also be added to the list, since communism from the time of the Russian Revolution to the time of its implosion in the 1980s spanned just a fraction more than a half-century. Today, some say that our own country's military adventurism in Vietnam, Afghanistan, and Iraq may be following the same historical pattern. The obvious conclusion that can be drawn from these examples is that military supremacy as an enduring manifestation of power does not guarantee longevity. Indeed, when military supremacy is used only to instill fear in those who have been conquered or occupied, the seeds of resistance have already been planted. At a certain point the conquered will hate what they fear more than they fear it and will then rebel.

Even those who continue to believe in military superiority as an emblem of national greatness are forced to admit that such supremacy in our era is finally synonymous with technological superiority—not valor or the customarily esteemed virtues of the warrior. But even technological superiority extracts a price in human terms. In a prophetic book entitled *Of Flight and Life* that he wrote in his later years, Charles Lindbergh described an incident when he was piloting a Lockheed Lightning P-38 back from a raid on Palau in the South Pacific. Flying in formation with three other P-38s, he was suddenly attacked by a Zero. The Japanese pilot had completely surprised Lindbergh and would have shot him down had not the other three pilots joined the battle and saved him. The incident taught Lindbergh that he had survived because the Lightning was a better plane than the Zero, which could not outmaneuver the American pilots. But he concluded years afterward that a victory guaranteed by science was not sufficient since "in worshipping science man gains power but loses the quality of life." And he added presciently: "Was science's power of survival only temporary, capable of winning battles but not of saving man?"

Of course, history demonstrates also that power conceived only as force (technological or otherwise) has often been bested by prowess, luck, or guile, which proves that military power has other opponents besides counterpower. Prowess: the slow and weighty warships of the Spanish Armada were regarded in their era as invincible. But they proved no match for the lighter and more maneuverable vessels commanded by Sir Francis Drake, who became their nemesis. Luck: in the battle of Tarawa in World War II, the Japanese commander was killed purely by chance before the invasion by an incoming round while he was moving from one post to another. From then on the Japanese forces on the island were leaderless at the top. The fierce battle lasted for three days, but the outcome was never in doubt because the Japanese were left without a central command. Guile: according to Homer and Virgil, the Trojan War had been fought over ten years to a standstill when Odysseus convinced the Greeks to conceal soldiers inside a huge wooden horse, which would be offered as a gift to the Trojans. If the Trojans brought the horse within the walls of Troy, the concealed soldiers could emerge and open the gates of the city to the main Greek force. The ruse worked, and Troy fell. Call it guile, if you wish, but the victory was one of intelligence over strength. For a more contemporary parallel in guile consider the heavyweight title match between Muhammad Ali and George Foreman in Zaire. For eight rounds, Ali permitted himself to be pummeled by Foreman in what came to be called the "rope-a-dope" strategy. The more powerful of the two, Foreman punched and punched until he was spent. At that point, Ali struck, and the fight was over. Again, a victory of intelligence over strength.

Speaking of intelligence, how can the enriching of natural intelligence in the quest for knowledge not be regarded as one of the most powerful factors in what is called human progress? From the time of the invention of the wheel to the advanced surgical skill that permitted a surgeon recently to remove cataracts from both my eyes, insert crystal lenses, and reward me with 20/20 vision with no need for glasses, the power of knowledge is an enduring history of possibilities that became facts. And their staying power—their ability to endure—has become as beneficial as it is indisputable, not only in scientific terms (medicine, architecture, aeronautics, agriculture, and so on) but in the human disciplines and the arts as well. What gives literature its staying power but its affirmation of the permanent truths of human nature and its capacity to touch the human spirit everywhere and at any time? Why are plays such as *Medea* and *Antigone* still in repertory after two thousand years but solid proof that a woman wronged by her husband is capable of deeds far beyond our imagining or that a sister who has to choose between love of her brother and compliance with an arbitrary state regulation will choose love even if her choice results in her own death? Why are the *Iliad* and the *Odyssey* still read but that they show how life always means a departure from home, a struggle with whatever forces await us (in war, in education, in business, in politics), and then end in a return to the home we left? Why does the tragedy of *Romeo and Juliet* still resonate but for the fact that we sympathize and identify ourselves with lovers who come together by choice and not to accommodate a family's or a community's wishes? And who among us cannot identify with what the anonymous Anglo-Saxon author of *The Seafarer* wrote about the risks of sailing: "But there isn't a man on earth so proud, / So born to greatness, so bold in his youth, / Grown so brave, or so graced by God, / That he feels no fear as the sails unfurl, / Wondering what fate has willed or will do"?

Perhaps it was for this reason that Ezra Pound, from whose translation of *The Seafarer* from Old English I have excerpted these few lines, could and did say that all poetry is contemporary, which frankly means that the ongoing presence of poetry in particular and literature in general has no past tense. That is where the power of literature lies—in the presence that words create when they are read or heard. And that presence is invariably undeniable and enduring. One need not be a sailor to sense what the author of *The Seafarer* is implying, namely, that fate never absolves us of our fear of the possible no matter how pride, destiny, youth, bravery, or blessedness has favored us. That fear is universal, and we recognize and feel it in the poet's words. This is what Robert Frost confirmed when he wrote: "The right reader of a good poem can tell the moment it strikes him that he has taken an immortal wound, that he will never get over it. That is to say, permanence in poetry as in love is perceived instantly. It has not to wait the test of time. The proof of a poem is not that we have never forgotten it, but that we knew at sight that we never could forget it."

This naturally leads to a consideration of the power of education since it is as a result of education that we were exposed to those subjects upon which our culture rests—poetry, of course, included. We were first educated by our upbringers, who taught us everything from basic hygiene to good manners. Then came professional teachers from whom we learned the basics—the American language, history, mathematics, the natural and social sciences, the disciplines of various sports, and so on. After high school, when we would no longer be pupils but voluntary learners or students, there would be more history, more literature, more science, and the rest of the canon. I am speaking here of liberal education, where truth is pursued for its own sake and where our natural appetite to know is an end in itself. This is where minds are born, and the power of teachers to put such minds in motion is in fact the gift of gifts. Once in motion the mind seeks truth at its own momentum, pursues it to its multiple sources, rids itself of superstition, and seeks the ultimate prize—intellectual freedom. The seeker is then truly liberated and lives the life of a free man. It is relevant here to be reminded that the word *libera* in Latin—from which we derive words such as "liberty" and "liberal"—is in turn derived from the Latin word for book, *liber,* which suggests that the Romans saw a connection between books and independence of mind, between learning and freedom.

Teachers who champion and spur independence of thought possess (often without their being aware of it) the power to inspire. At the University of Notre Dame there were great teachers such as Father Leo R. Ward, Frank O'Malley, Richard Sullivan, John T. Frederick, Thomas Stritch, and others, and their names are enshrined in the minds of those students who were empowered and emancipated by them. And there have been inspiring teachers since, including presidents John J. Cavanaugh, Theodore M. Hesburgh, Edward A. Malloy, and John I. Jenkins, each of whom is known as both a priest and an educator first and foremost. If a student in his college career is fortunate enough to have one or two such inspiring teachers, as opposed to qualified academicians, he should consider himself lucky. The impact of Frank O'Malley on his students has been well documented in memoirs, essays, and biographies since his death in 1974. Perhaps the greatest tribute was the number of his former students who attended a three-day retrospective for O'Malley in the early 1990s. Ken Woodward, then an editor at *Newsweek* and an O'Malley veteran, brought the event to national notice in the magazine. As one of the attendees, I heard a story about O'Malley that I would like to think is true. It was widely known that O'Malley's devotion to his students was sacrosanct. Teaching was his primary mission in life, as his sister verified during the conference, even though he combined it with editorial work and the writing of occasional essays. But he never published the "big book." After his death, a friend was asked to inspect his bachelor quarters on campus in Dillon Hall. He found on one side of O'Malley's bed a number of books published by his former students, including *The Last Hurrah*, which its author, Edward O'Connor, dedicated to O'Malley. On the other side of the bed was a collection of the best papers written by former students dating back to 1936. Under the bed was a shoebox filled with uncashed checks made out to O'Malley from students to whom he had "lent" money when they were in need as undergraduates. After graduation they paid him back by check, but he never cashed even one. To many who heard the story it was evident that the "big book" was in that shoebox. But the point that is confirmed by Frank O'Malley's life is the powerful bond that exists (and continues to exist) between teacher and generations of that teacher's students. It is a spiritual power, and it is immortal.

For many years there was a swimming coach at Notre Dame named Gil Burdick. Not an academic in the traditional sense, he taught basic and advanced swimming for decades (swimming was a requirement). I was one of the students who benefited from his tutelage. Upon reflection I have often asked myself (and have so said in public on several occasions) how many lives did Gil Burdick save after his swimmers were graduated. And how many other lives did he save when those he taught taught others? That presents itself as quite a legacy. History is rife with similar legacies of teachers whose names survive not in bronze entablature but in the lives of those who were the beneficiaries of those who generously shared their knowledge: Socrates, Tertullian, Minucius Felix, Erasmus, Bernard of Clairvaux, John Henry Newman, Robert Maynard Hutchins, Mark Van Doren, William Sloane Coffin, and Sarah Johnston.

Sarah Johnston, you say? Never heard of her. How does she deserve to be listed among the luminaries? This is how. Tom Lincoln, the father of Abraham and Sarah Lincoln, lost his wife, Nancy Hanks, to a cattle-borne transmittable "milk disease" when Abraham was nine years old and his sister only slightly older. Being a dawn-to-dusk farmer, Tom Lincoln desperately needed someone to rear his two children. He was told of a widow named Sarah Johnston, who lived in Kentucky with three children of her own. In due course, Tom Lincoln went to Kentucky, proposed to Sarah Johnston, and brought her and her two daughters and son back to his farm in Indiana. There she developed a special love for Abraham Lincoln, taught him to read and write, and gave him his first books—*Pilgrim's Progress, Aesop's Fables,* and the King James version of the Bible. Had Nancy Hanks lived, she certainly would not have been capable of giving the boy what Sarah Johnston gave him since she as well as Tom Lincoln were illiterate. In retrospect, we can rightly wonder what would have happened to Abraham Lincoln without Sarah Johnston. He probably would have remained a farmer like his father. He certainly could not have been a lawyer, a congressman, or the president of the United States had it not been for the love and tutelage he received from Sarah Johnston. And had Lincoln not been president at the time of the Civil War, the United States of America might not be the country as we know it today. And all of this was because of the love and care that one woman had for a son who was not even her own. And yet, despite the debt that all Americans owe to Sarah Johnston, too few people know who she was. My guess is that Sarah Johnston would really make light of this. Like all who act out of selflessness and love, she undoubtedly regarded her affection for Lincoln as an end in itself, proving that love is its own reward. But the powerful consequences of that love outlived both Sarah Johnston and Lincoln himself and have repercussions to this day in the lives of all Americans and anyone else conversant with American history.

In a recent feature article in *Newsweek,* Jon Meacham stated that the word for power in Latin is *imperium.* This enforced the basic theme of his article in which he concluded that power or *imperium* was "at heart the capacity to bend reality to your will." The inevitable conclusion that one is forced to draw from Meacham's thesis is that power is ultimately coercive. Whether achieved by force, money, deception, seduction, or training, the aim is to compel people to do what you want them to do. If this sounds more than vaguely fascistic, the reason is that it is. My belief is that genuine power is derivative in the fullest sense not from *imperium* but from the Latin verb *potere* and its French descendant *poeir* (eventually *pouvoir*). The meaning of power here can best be translated as "to be able" or "to enable." The imperial meaning of power as coercion is not even implied. In this sense the enabling of Lincoln by Sarah Johnston fully qualifies as the true meaning of power. Hers was a selfless act of sharing what she knew with young Lincoln and making it possible for him to continue to learn as he grew, relying on the basic skills and appetite that she had instilled and awakened in him. It is the same impulse that motivates parents and teachers at all levels of education, and its power can never be underestimated.

I would argue that this same transformative power is one of the many beneficial capabilities of the arts, particularly the arts of music and poetry. Both music and poetry seem to have the power of putting those who are exposed to them in touch with their deeper selves. How this happens is truly a mystery, but we know that it does happen when the imagination of someone is inspired to manifest itself in song or words so that the listeners or readers are changed by the experience. Consider the esteem in which the French chanteuse Edith Piaf was held by the French people before, during, and after World War II. Physical beauty had nothing to do with her appeal. Here was a woman who was not called "the little sparrow" for nothing; she was diminutive, eschewed opulent wardrobes on stage, and seemed indifferent to cosmetics. But she had an unignorable and quintessentially Parisian voice that was the voice of France for more than a half-century, and she holds a permanent place in the French pantheon of song that can only be described as timeless. Her death had such a crushing effect on the internationally famous author

Jean Cocteau that he said he no longer wished to live. And Cocteau and others listened to Edith Piaf as others do to this day because of something in her songs that touched and still touches them.

The same can be said of the legendary Egyptian singer Om Khalsoum. She was revered not only in Egypt but also in Lebanon, Syria, Jordan, Iraq, Saudi Arabia, Yemen, the Emirates, and across North Africa. Her appeal was to women as well as to men, but particularly to men, who seemed almost mesmerized by her songs. She had created the custom of presenting a concert once a month in an open-theater on the banks of the Nile. By midafternoon on the day of the concert many businesses, stores, and government offices would close so that the owners and employees could ready themselves spiritually for the evening. It was said, not quite in jest, that if she were invited by an Arab head of state to perform in his country and refused the invitation, then the government would collapse on the following day. When she died, it was a time of national mourning among all the Arabic-speaking peoples and beyond. And as a final tribute, it was estimated that more than 4 million (4,000,000!) people came to her funeral in Cairo.

Like music, poetry has the same irresistible power to awaken the self that exists deeply within each one of us. Like music, its true power is the power to endure unforgettably. It would not be far-fetched to claim that words spoken or written so as to qualify as poems are actually immortal. They not only never die, but they also stay alive in their original form. Many whose lives are "immortalized" by having buildings, colleges, airports, ships, towns, or even whole cities named after them cannot rival the immortality that a poet's words bestow upon the poet who wrote them. Solomon's "Song of Songs" possesses a passion and an eroticism that is timeless. And what of William Shakespeare? All we know of Shakespeare historically is the rather thin biography that scholars have given us. But in his thirty-seven plays, his superb sonnets, and the additional poems we have Shakespeare in full, sometimes in the characters of his plays and at other times directly. If we did not have the plays and the poetry, Shakespeare would be just a name parenthesized between 1564 and 1616. But his words survive and transcend the time and place of their creation so that they resonate with people everywhere and at all times.

As a matter of personal endorsement of this statement, I knew a foreign author who told me years ago that the only reason he learned English was so that he could read Shakespeare in the original.

During the months when I was preparing to write this essay, I became more and more inclined to the view that power conceived of as force to achieve supremacy or control was in essence related to pride, vanity, and egotism. I am not naïve enough to believe that force is not sometimes required in human or national relations. Police work and acts of self-defense often justifiably necessitate the use of force. But unless we choose to live in a Hobbesian world where men are regarded as mutually predatory and where power in its most violent forms is seen as the final arbiter, I believe that a more enlightened norm of power should be preferred and extolled. This is the power that I associate with education, love, and the liberal and fine arts. The sharing of knowledge has a beneficial effect upon both the teacher and the taught, and its ultimate benefits are incalculable. The power of love—fraternal, conjugal, or communal—is at heart the mother and father of trust without which social life is impossible. And finally the liberal and fine arts "enable" men to fulfill their personal and creative natures in ways that simply do not die. Contrasted with power that possesses these attributes, power that is allied with militarism, money, class, race, or science, however triumphant it may appear and however long it may prevail, is by nature finite and secondary.

T H R E E

Strike Down the Band

I begin on a personal note. My son majored in music education at Duquesne University and was graduated with a citation as the most outstanding senior in that field. After graduation he went on to teach in two different high-school music education programs. Then I shared with him a grim period when the music education programs in which he was involved both as a teacher and band director were cut back, minimized, or otherwise unnecessarily disturbed. The question I asked then and ask now is, Why, when economies are called for, are the arts the first to be targeted? Instead of striking up the bands in our country, why are we determined to strike them down—and all in the name of prudence and fiscal wisdom? Let us remember that the word "economics" comes from the Greek word meaning "house management." What kind of good house management is it to deprive a family of that which is central to its cultural life in the name, let us remember, of economics? Above all, why should music be the first to be evicted, for heaven's sake? Why not science, mathematics, hygiene, and so on? I've asked this question many times, and I am asking it now. Personally I'm against any cuts in education across the board, but I have yet to receive an intelligent explanation that justifies penalizing students by depriving them of an artistic education, especially in music. I think I would be somewhat pacified if those who advocate things such as the death of music programs would be willing to drop music from their own lives as totally as they would wish it done in the schools—no stereo in the home, no opera, no symphonies, no jazz, no music in the car, no CDs, no singing in the shower, no music whatever.

The absurdity of this suggestion answers itself. Unless you are a total troglodyte, a life without music is like a life without sublimity. If it is difficult for a normal adult to imagine a life *sans* music, then why is not the cutting out of music programs from the educational curriculum regarded with indignation, shock, and even rage? Is it because the so-called practical programs and technology-related studies are regarded as being ultimately more lucrative? Whether this is true or not, is it the business of educators to permit ends (commercial or otherwise) to justify means? On the contrary, is it not the responsibility of true educators to resist trendy pressures and enticements and stand up for those values that enhance a student's imaginative and cultural life regardless of what consequences this may have in later life? In other words, does it square with education itself to eliminate what any intelligent educator or administrator would be forced to acknowledge as the heart of education itself, namely, the nurturing of the imagination?

Thomas Jefferson, who not only was what we already know he was—president of the United States, president and founder of the University of Virginia, framer of the Virginia statutes, author of the Declaration of Independence—but also an inventor, a musician, and the author of poetry in English, Latin, and Greek, believed that a total education was rooted in memory, reason, and imagination. Translated into a curriculum, this means schooling in history, philosophy, and the arts. This is not vocational training. This is not the in-servicing of technicians. This is not graduating people who believe that the world began when they were born. This is not readying people for the status quo or the temporarily relevant. (Nazism, fascism, and communism, we must remember, were temporarily relevant at one time, and whole generations were schooled in their doctrines to their eternal tragedy.) This is not short-changing people of those disciplines that mark a liberally educated man or woman, but educating them to be aware that the present grows out of the past, that logical thinking and arriving at just judgments are what minds exist to do, that dreaming or imagining the world anew and then realizing those imaginings are what makes living a daily and ongoing drama of creation.

As much as I respect history and right reasoning, I must admit that I am partial to the imagination. Why? Because I believe that everything—repeat, everything—originates there. I referred earlier to the Declaration of Independence. Where did it originate except in Thomas Jefferson's imagination? Where did Shakespeare's plays originate except in Shakespeare's imagination? We can trace Disney World to one man who years ago imagined a cartoon involving a talking mouse named Mickey. This in time created the whole empire. Where does everything from the languages we speak or write down to the way we are dressed right now originate but in the imagination of the many, the few, or you or me? The imagination is the primal source of all that we do. And it is only the arts—dance, painting, poetry, music, and so on—that permit the imagination to mature. And yet, amazingly, it is the arts that have been made the undeserved and unexpected enemies of those who really do not have the imaginative good of students at heart. For such people, I am forced to admit, money is god, especially money saved or money spent only on utilitarian needs. They believe that saving money by depriving the arts of funding, especially government funding, is simply good bottom-line thinking.

Let me insert at this point that the attitude of many in the arts is that such bottom-liners must be placated and schmoozed so that they will be inclined to loosen their purse strings. (Actually it is not *their* purse strings, after all, since it is not their money we are talking about; it is ours, the people's.) This attitude is misguided and demeaning. Pray you avoid it. The French, when confronted with what cannot be avoided but still must be dealt with, rely on being "correct." As long as we must, let us imitate the French and deal with the circumstances as correctly as we can. But the ultimate goal of those who believe in the synchronicity of government and the arts is the electoral defeat of those representatives who presently stand in opposition to this alliance. Their defeat and removal from the national scene cannot come too soon. And simultaneously we should work diligently to repeal and refute those attitudes that the art-haters have already created in the public mind.

Let us remember John Kennedy's answer to his brother Robert when Robert suggested that they make a deal with then Senator Lyndon Johnson prior to the vote for the 1960 presidential nomination in order to eliminate Johnson as an opponent. John Kennedy disagreed. He told his brother, "Let's defeat him, then deal with him." This is exactly what he did, and it's the political model we should follow. We cannot forget that we are dealing for the most part with shallow people. Some would call them inferior people, even dangerous people. How should one regard those who work for the elimination of music from our educational curriculum, for example? Here is William Shakespeare from a scene in *The Merchant of Venice* on the subject:

> The man that hath no music in himself,
> Nor is not mov'd with concord of sweet sounds,
> Is fit for treason, stratagems, and spoils;
> The motions of his spirit are dull as night,
> And his affections dark as Erebus.
> Let no such man be trusted.

Shakespeare's attitude does not leave much room for compromise. Bottom-liners would certainly not applaud Shakespeare in this context. And if the bottom line were everything, such people would be hard to refute. But the bottom line is not everything. There is such a thing as the top line, rarely mentioned but much more important. Without the top line, there would be no bottom line. The top line is concerned with visions, not costs; with potentiality, not restriction; with courage, not cowardice; with support, not suppression—with what is in the best interest of the young, regardless of the bearable burden it places on their elders. Fathers and mothers who sacrifice for their children would have no argument with this; they would understand its meaning immediately. They know what it is to sacrifice for the good of their children, and they know what the consequences would be if they didn't. Why can we not expect the same spirit from those who are elected and entrusted with the public good?

The bottom-liners often fall back on the argument that schooling is brief in the context of a lifetime, and that a person's real life begins only when he leaves school. They say that earning is more important than learning. After all, they say, a good two-thirds of a person's expected lifetime of some sixty years, plus or minus, is spent in the all-important business of earning. This sounds convincing. This sounds obvious. But it is basically a lie.

Let's look at this life formula accurately. In an expected life span of sixty years, we do spend approximately a third or twenty-some years in formal education. We also spend another third asleep (calculated on the basis of approximately eight hours a day). Then we spend the remaining third as earners. That's the mathematically accurate way of looking at life. And any parent or educator or even a disinterested observer will concede that learning precedes, determines, and even dictates the eventual manner of our earning. If we educate people "on the cheap," what can we expect but a cheapened adult population in a cheapened society governed by cheapening national policies and attitudes?

I believe that the cheapening of our national values must be reversed. Let those who say that the government should get out of our lives, who believe that government should be of and by but not for the people, who frown on anything in the national budget that is not related to our national defense, who believe in the elimination of Social Security and other programs that have served and continue to serve the public good, who say that the National Endowment for the Arts and the complementary National Endowment for the Humanities should be eliminated or only tokenly funded—let these people reread the Preamble to the Constitution, which stipulates that civic leadership should "provide for the common defense, promote the general Welfare, and secure the Blessings of Liberty to ourselves and our Posterity." I contend that nothing promotes the general welfare and seeks the blessings of liberty better than the arts—even more than religions, which, for some reason in our time, tend more toward divisiveness than unity. And of all the arts, music stands alone as the ultimate unifier—the one art, according to the great Mexican muralist David Alfaro Siqueiros, without the need of translation, *la única arte sin discriminación.*

I think it is regrettable that many who believe in the importance and even the indispensability of music in the formal education of students often feel compelled to defend it in terms of how it enhances life in other areas, which music certainly does. But music is not Muzak. Music is not important because it is an aid to purchasing while people are looking over the pork chops or picking out underwear. Nor is it important because we have the results of one test among many, which demonstrates that students who listened to Mozart for ten minutes before taking a standard IQ spatial reasoning test finished eight points higher than students who did not listen to Mozart. All of this is relevant, of course, and it is interesting as far as it goes, but music needs no justification for its existence other than that existence itself. Does the beautiful need any other justification outside of itself? The hunger for beauty, like the hunger for music and for knowledge and for God, is part of our very natures. We don't listen to music out of duty. We listen to it because we like it; it touches us. We don't learn because our learning will some day "pay off." We learn because it fulfills us, satisfies our curiosity, delivers us from ignorance. And that's enough. By constantly seeking to justify music as utilitarian instead of an end in itself, we fall into endless disquisition. Defending liberal education in the 1950s, Yale's then president, A. Whitney Griswold, said, "We spend so much time defending what we practice that we have no time to practice what we're defending." Substitute music for liberal education in this quote, and you have a description of much of what occupies many of us today.

I believe that educating students with an appreciation for music or, better yet, with the talent and skill to *make* music is one of the crowns of learning. I cite the example of my own son, to whom I have already referred. For years he taught music, then turned to composing, and is now one of the leading composers for wind symphonies both in the United States and abroad. Much of this is traceable to his undergraduate and graduate years as a student of music.

Like poetry, music puts us in touch with our feelings and, through our feelings, with our very souls. Being in touch with one's self, being capable of being alone and enjoying one's own company for a time, being moved to feel what one would not otherwise feel—how can any intelligent parent, teacher, or, above all, political representative find fault with this? On the contrary, are these not goals that should be abundantly and continually supported?

In this connection, how can any government feel truly patriotic while spending approximately half of its annual budget on the defense of its freedom and culture and way of life and not spend even 1 percent of that same budget to nurture the freedom and culture and way of life that it claims to be defending? Is it not a national shame that the chairman of the National Endowment for the Arts or any other of the supporters of the NEA should come like mendicants before panels or committees that would think nothing of enlarging our fleet of Stealth bombers ($1,500,000,000 per bomber) or of replicating the *SS Ticonderoga* ($14,000,000,000) while approving something in the area of $100,500,000 for the National Endowment for the Arts, and grudgingly at that, since the attitude of many of this ilk is that the National Endowment for the Arts should be scrapped anyway. That figure of $100,500,000 is one-tenth the cost of one Stealth bomber—the price of the landing gear, perhaps, and of some of its highly sophisticated software. That $100,500,000 for the NEA factors down to 35 cents per taxpaying citizen per year. Canada and Sweden, with populations of 28 million and 7 million, respectively, tag approximately 10 percent of their national budgets for the arts. Putting comparisons aside, I recently heard David McCulloch remind us that 65 percent of taxpaying Americans would be willing to give as much as $5 a year to the arts. Are the enemies of art listening? If not, why not? If so, why don't they get immediately in step with the will of the real government, the only government—the people?

Contributing to the arts really is contributing to our national wealth. Not doing so, as one student of mine succinctly expressed it, is engaging in a conspiracy against our own greatness. And it is this greatness, past and present, that defines American culture at its best. It is what we have to share with one another and the world. What do we do for those who study here, or who merely visit our country, but expose them to the national heroes of our past and present who have created our architecture, our poetry and literature, our fine arts, our music? Particularly, our music.

Excising music programs from our educational and cultural life is not only shortsighted, it is suicidal. Repeat, suicidal. We are literally killing our spiritual selves if we do so, or if we remain silent while others do so. The enemies of art will tell you that government has no business in the arts and that the private sector will fulfill this need. I, for one, take nothing away from the private sector. Without such philanthropy, where would we be? The private sector has done much, and it deserves our gratitude. But forget the adjective for the moment (private) and think only of the noun (sector). The assumption is that part of our society—a sector or section—will assume the cultural burden of all of society. No one in the private sector thinks that this is possible or desirable. On the contrary, they hold, as I do, that federal funding—encompassing all the states—will help as many component parts as possible, parts that would never have a chance to be funded otherwise. Only a governmental agency can have the entire country as its agenda, and rightly so. It seems to me that only the narrow-minded or the just plain stingy would deny this. But then, at heart, that may be just what we are dealing with—stingy people. Their problem may just be the age-old problem of the greedy. They are tight when they should be munificent.

America remains a great country, despite our current crop of problems, because its promise created what no other country in history was able to create. It is on the side of the imagination. Its population can best be likened to an orchestra where individual players contribute to the ongoing music of our lives and where the whole is always greater than its parts. As educators we know that orchestras don't just happen. To exist and grow they require instruction, discipline, practice, know-how, and love. If we love our country as we love our students or our families, then we will dedicate ourselves to such instruction, discipline, practice, know-how, and love. If we ourselves do not have the knowledge or talent to do so, we will and should support those who do. And the governments we elect—those who should represent our best interests and sow the seeds of our future good—should be no less dedicated in their willingness to do so as well.

The late poet John Ciardi once said that you judge a man by what engages his attention. This can be transposed easily to state that you can judge a nation and a people by what engages their attention. Let us hope that it will be said of us that our attention was engaged by the best that is known and thought in the world, of which music—that which relates to love in harmony and system, as Plato described it—is the deserved and deserving queen.

FOUR

The Lasting Marriage of Knowledge and Belief

My goal is to identify where a Catholic university can and should assert its identity as such, never in a dogmatic or canonical way but in the exploratory spirit that is characteristic of all who believe that the search for truth and the correlative spirit of human freedom are inseparable. I am referring here to the university as John Henry Newman and many of his successors have defined it—an institution where truth is sought and shared for its own sake. This is not the sense in which it is perceived in John Paul II's *Ex Corde Ecclesiae.* It is important to establish at the outset that the search for truth and organizational or doctrinal conformity can never be synonymous in a true university, if for no other reason than that the university must defend the search for truth wherever it leads even if that search ends in "apparent error," that is, a deviation from what is regarded as official or traditional truth or truths. Often the "apparent error" may eventually be accepted as a corrective for or even a replacement of certain "truths" that were once unquestioningly believed as true when in fact they were not. There is a long history of such replacements, including the long-standing perception of the earth as flat until it was seen as round.

In the university the whole concept of tenure exists primarily to protect those who are involved in this search for similar correctives at the frontiers of knowledge. Creating a conflict between this principle and so-called official positions would put any bishop as well as the administration and faculty of a Catholic university at irreconcilable odds vis-à-vis academic freedom. A similar conflict could arise from the encyclical's insistence that the administration and faculty at Catholic universities or colleges should be Catholic. Experience has shown repeatedly that those of a variety of different confessions among the administration and faculty at Catholic universities and colleges have supported the goals of Catholic education in the most catholic sense—in some cases more assuredly than nominal Catholics have. A university is not a seminary, after all, and different criteria apply.

A Catholic university can, should, and must do as well as or better than what any nonsectarian university can do in the studies of arts and letters, the social sciences, and the natural sciences. (I leave professional or vocational courses out of this list since they are not at the heart of liberal education as I understand it, and liberal education for me is the heart of university life.) But doing as well or better is not enough. It must also do or attempt to do what any nonsectarian university by law cannot do. In other words, it must—whenever it is relevant—explore the relation of theological truth to subjects in the curriculum across the board. If a Catholic institution of higher learning presumes that its responsibility to theological inquiry is fulfilled simply by offering theological courses without relating the implications of theology to the rest of the curriculum, it is not doing what it should be doing. Once theology is regarded as being hermetically unrelated to other subjects, then students can never have the formal occasions for asking the questions that will develop the ethically centered collegiate conscience for which a Catholic university exists to awaken and nurture. How else can students examine the relationship between belief and philosophy, belief and history, belief and the social sciences (including economics), belief and scientific thought, and, above all, belief and literature? If a Catholic university ignores or marginalizes this basic and ongoing inquiry, no matter how much it encourages a life of prayer or the commendable doing of good deeds in society, such as working summers in Appalachia, then it is abandoning the main reason for its existence as a university. To take refuge in the justification that the dissemination and interchange of knowledge are sufficient is to assume that knowledge, though certainly an end in itself, has no relationship to anything other than itself. Those universities and colleges that believe—and there are many—that knowledge is virtue (*scientia est virtus*) know that this is false. There are as many knowledgeable sycophants, liars, slanderers, murderers, and connivers as there are ignorant ones. Knowledge that is not integrated into a spiritual scale of values is not virtuous at all; it is simply neutral. It can be directed toward whatever the knower chooses, and what is that end answerable to except the values of the knower? Likewise, if belief and knowledge exist in a vacuum with neither one acknowledging the other, it is not long before belief degenerates into blind faith (fideism) or even into superstition.

I have neither the wisdom nor the time to investigate the relationship between belief and all the subjects in a college curriculum, but I am certain of one thing, and that is that I cannot think of one subject where the ultimate questions can be answered by the disciplines of that subject alone. Why? Because the final questions are invariably ethical, and ethics derives from a theological base, and such a base can be a common reference for all. For example, in medical science or in the natural sciences as a whole, is the scientifically possible always permissible? If not, why not? If so, why? Think of cloning, of Jack Kevorkian's views on euthanasia, of abortion, of indiscriminate strip mining, of unchecked nuclear power in war or peace, of deforestation or pollution. In economics, why did it take so many so long to recognize as a sham the ideology of communism when its fundamental flaw was apparent to any thinker who was sensitive to the sacredness of private property; and why, when the system failed, was there so much surprise? Contrarily, is unrestrained capitalism the salvation of the American way of life, or, as the history of monopolies and the robber barons reveals, is this merely a euphemism for greed on a corporate scale, and to hell with those it victimizes? Is there an ethical problem with profit and the whole matter of the profit motive? Think of the eventual social consequences when theory translates into practice. We are all familiar with CEOs who make astronomical salaries while the workers who created such profits in the first place are unrewarded, underpaid, or simply fired. In political matters, when is any country, including our own, justified in committing its citizenry to war; and is total war against armies, navies, air forces, and civilians alike ever justified? Does majority rule make the decisions of the majority right or merely so?

And, sociologically speaking, what about the recent fudging of ethnic heritage and constitutional allegiance, as in Italo-American, Irish-American, or Afro-American? Is this kind of hyphenation what one puts down on one's passport when one is traveling abroad, or is "American" sufficient? If this is sufficient abroad, why isn't it sufficient at home? Wouldn't Thomas Jefferson ask any such hyphenated citizen to make up his or her mind and then remind either one that this country has no blood base and that ethnicity and political allegiance were never equated in the Constitution, despite the reactionism of the Ku Klux Klan and the Aryan Nation? Who, for example, ever thinks of Jefferson as Welsh-American? This is not just an academic question since we know that tribalism, when mixed with constitutional allegiance, often has moral as well as political consequences. In psychological matters, is it wise to attempt to explain human behavior only in terms of one doctrinaire school of thought to the exclusion of all others, or is it wiser to see some wisdom in all in a spirit of genuine catholicity? Freud, for example, says that sexual desire is co-terminous with life itself. It is always there, and it is never totally or permanently satisfied or satisfiable. This tension, in Freud's view, is the dynamism of life itself. Isn't this more in conformity with everyone's experience than the views of those who ally themselves with total suppression, total indulgence, or total sublimation?

But it is literature and its study that is at the heart of this question of knowledge and values since it is from literature and from literature alone that students are introduced "feelingly" into the real dramas of life. Why? Because literature is what Newman said it was— "the autobiography of man." Moreover, it is where students (and readers generally) really experience and become sensitive to the dilemmas of the human heart and soul in conflict with themselves.

This is literature's domain, and it resonates with every human being's daily destiny. In moments of inexpressible joy, sorrow, anger, or anguish we turn to the world's great writers (especially poets) to confirm our right to feel what we feel.

What one finds in great literature is what T. S. Eliot called "a sense of the genuine." He was not speaking of writing that was polemical or devotional but of writing that encompassed the whole of human nature, where human beings were seen as capable of degeneration as of redemption and where the writer's tragic sense enabled him to know the difference and to describe each as such. It is also what enables students of literature (critics and readers) to recognize when even great writers come up short in their testaments of human endeavor. Take Ernest Hemingway, for example. In novels such as *A Farewell to Arms, For Whom the Bell Tolls,* and *The Old Man and the Sea,* Hemingway left us superb portraits of love, tragedy, and valor, but his admiration for bullfighting may have caused him to confuse bravado with courage, which he correctly defined as "grace under pressure." He never identified the purpose of such "grace under pressure," apparently assuming that courage, even when purposeless, was admirable in itself. Whereas Aristotle defined courage as what enables one to do what is right, Hemingway extolled the courage of matadors who, like boxers and other professional athletes, do what they do, after all, for money. Hemingway only focused on tauromachical skill. He ignored the fact that bullfighting in Spain rewarded bullfighters handsomely. Juan Belmonte, in the year when Babe Ruth earned a season-long salary of $80,000, received $62,000 for a single *corrida.* Certainly he exhibited "grace under pressure," but it was not all ritual. Greed had a hand in it as well.

Consider, too, how what was once regarded both socially and ecclesiastically as the norm for marriage is now regarded as regressive, even inimical to love between man and woman. I am speaking of arranged marriages versus marriages based on freedom of choice. In *Romeo and Juliet,* Shakespeare pitted the two traditions against one another and dramatized the tragic consequences. But why is this a tragedy? In parts of India, for example, where arranged marriages are not uncommon, Juliet would probably be regarded as an ornery girl who got what she deserved because she disobeyed her parents.

Shakespeare was relying on a response closer to the truth of the human heart. But that came about after centuries of correctives and replacements, beginning with the minstrelsy of the Arabs, the translations of this tradition through the troubadours from Andalusia to Europe, the evolution of the laws of courtly love, and eventually the triumph of the belief that love and choice are indivisible. The literary consequences form a direct line from Dante's Beatrice to *West Side Story.*

In contemporary terms a sensitivity to genuine literature permits us to ask what our critical response should be when literary worth is equated almost exclusively with gender, ethnic heritage, race, or any of various marginal lifestyles. Isn't it an ethical or theological dimension that permits us to see through such irrelevance? Doesn't it allow us to say that literature is not sociology and that real literature is written by those who transcend gender, ethnic heritage, race, or anything else in the quest for what Terence alluded to when he wrote: "Ego homo sum, et nihil humanum mihi alienum est" (I am human, and nothing human is alien to me)? Sociological or political considerations here are of secondary concern if they are of any concern at all. What is primary is what is on the page, and Eliot's insight into how this should be evaluated is no less relevant than his aforementioned comment on genuineness: "The greatness of literature cannot be determined only by literary standards; though we must remember that whether it is literature or not can be determined only by literary standards."

Regardless of how the theological or ethical dimensions of a variety of subjects are explored in what is called "higher learning," it should be accepted and expected at the outset that there will be controversy. Indeed, the very nature of university life (and public life in general) is that it is controversial. Civility should govern all such disquisition, of course, but we should be under no illusions that controversy will be any less frequent or intense because of that, nor should it be. Obedience to the demands of the search for truth is the only obedience that should govern our efforts in this regard. And here we need to be reminded of the fact that truth is something that is rarely known in advance. John Donne put it this way in the third of his *Satires*:

> On a huge hill,
> Cragged, and steep, Truth stands, and he that will
> Reach her, about must, and about must go;
> And what the hill's suddenness resists, win so;
> Yet strive so, that before age, death's twilight,
> Thy soul rest, for none can work in that night.
> To will, implies delay, therefore now do.

Those who dogmatically insist on silencing or curtailing debate because they claim they already know the truth (both in essence and in application) are like those who insist they know the answer before they know the question, which is as silly as it sounds. I do not deny that certain essentialist values can be known in advance, namely, that murder is wrong, that obsessive resistance to evil is often, as *Moby-Dick* reveals to us, an evil in itself and ultimately self-destructive, that love outlives death, and so forth. But it is at the intersection of essentialism and existentialism where the real drama of life happens and where choices with theological dimensions often must be made, and that has been my concern.

Robert Maynard Hutchins, when he was chancellor of the University of Chicago, gave an address whose very title conveys the spirit of what I have been attempting to describe: "We Must Be Locked in Vital Argument." In the life of the intellect the vitality of true argument is the nourishment that permits intellectual growth. But the argument should be vital, that is, it should be beyond ambition, campus politics, spite, or vindictiveness. Its subject should be life itself under whatever discipline it is studied. No more should be asked. No less should be accepted.

5

Belief and the Critic

The true relationship between Christianity and literary criticism has invariably been complicated by those who attempt to superimpose the nature of one completely upon the other. Such is the error of the dogmatist. But an equally fallacious and futile approach is to regard the problem as a touch-me-not, a problem better left unsolved for reasons foreign to both Christianity and literary criticism. The first error springs from misdirected enthusiasm or sheer ignorance, and the second from prejudice or intellectual cowardice or both. Each error avoids the reality of the problem and thus defers or actually prevents solution.

The analysis of the true relationship between Christianity and literary criticism remains an arduous literary endeavor despite the fact that Father Harold Gardiner, S.J., has established some laudable, practical standards for the evaluation of fiction, and even though speculative critics such as Martin Turnell, Maurice De Wulf, Jacques Maritain, and others have given us some provocative critical and aesthetic insights into the nature of this relationship. The extensive middle ground between the practical and predominantly moral tenets of Gardiner and the theories of Turnell, De Wulf, and Maritain still invites profitable exploration. What, for example, are the responsibilities of the Christian as scholar or as practical critic in other, or more, than a purely moral sense? What are the disciplines demanded of a Christian as an explicator? Are these various responsibilities and disciplines unique for him alone, or are they the common lot of all literary critics?

It will be my purpose to suggest that the Christian critic differs from other critics, if he differs at all, not so much in method as in sensibility. By "method" I mean the way in which the literary critic (any literary critic) masters and uses scholarly and critical apparatus to determine, for instance, textual validity and accuracy and to elucidate meanings in the work of words itself in language that is free of pointless and postured critical jargon. By "sensibility" I mean the critic's awareness to values in literature, that is, to insights into the human situation that are inherent in and derived from a literary experience. Although most considerations of sensibility and method are inextricably involved, I intend to suggest that problems related to method tend to challenge the Christian critic as critic while problems related to sensibility tend to challenge the Christian critic as Christian. Analogously speaking, problems of method may be related to genus, while problems of sensibility are related to specific difference.

It is a truism to say that solving problems of scholarship is pivotal to critical methodology. Problems of scholarship are usually the first ones to confront the critic. Some of these problems are included in the following definition of scholarship formulated by David Daiches. For Daiches, scholarship is that literary activity which "throws light on the social and biographical origins of a work, on the cultural environment out of which it sprang, and on the transmission of the text, and thus often enables the critic to understand in some degree how the work came to be written and to see more clearly the meanings of certain parts of the text." If Daiches's definition is correct, then every scholar, regardless of his faith or his school, faces the same disciplines. Scholarship in this sense merely sets the stage for practical literary criticism, and every scholar works, as he must, within the limits of his own honesty, accuracy, ingenuity, and perseverance with available materials. But the threshold of criticism has not yet been crossed. What is of primary importance at this first stage of methodology is simply the individual's diligence in research and the way in which he is able to interpret his research.

When problems of scholarship have been solved as far as evidence and facility will permit, the critic is then able to "practice" his art as an explicator. If practical criticism is considered as the explication of text in order to increase understanding and enhance appreciation of a work, it is necessary to consider the method of explication, on the one hand, and then the understanding created by the explication as evaluative, on the other. The former consideration is still a matter of methodology and is, according to my original distinctions, a matter of confronting the Christian critic as critic. But any consideration of explication as evaluative—a goal identified by W. K. Wimsatt, Jr., in "Explication as Criticism" as the critic's main "critical problem" since it is based on the need of advancing "understanding and value as far as possible in union"—necessarily involves a critic's awareness of values and thus challenges his sensibility. Matters relative to sensibility transcend methodology per se and challenge the Christian critic as Christian.

Explication considered purely as method is governed by two factors. I am assuming at this point that the explicator has been astute enough to avoid Messrs. Wimsatt and Beardsley's intentional and affective fallacies and to purge himself of the flaws that T. S. Eliot in *The Sacred Wood* ascribed to the criticism of Swinburne, Charles Whibley, and Paul Moore. In practice these two factors go together, but in theory the explicator's method is to consider the work as an organism in order to show "elements in the writing which combine to make its particular quality" (H. Coombes) and to consider "the significance of the attitude it is likely to arouse in the experienced and sensitive reader" (David Daiches). Although this statement smacks of generality, I suggest that all critics in the practice of their art must work this common clay.

Even though it is possible to isolate in theory the method of explication within the limits of these two principles, it is not difficult to see to which pole many modern critics have gravitated. Elucidation through an examination of what Coombes has called the "elements in the writing which combine to make its particular quality" has been the approach of numerous modern critics, and terms such as "tension," "paradox," and "symbolic action" have become the stock phrases of their trade. Such criticism, which contains much that is truly excellent despite the fact that poet-critics such as Karl Shapiro and Mark Van Doren found little to praise in it, is invariably directed toward a consideration, however partial, of how the poem "works" in the organic sense. Yet it is only to the extent that the critic's sensibility suffuses such an approach that his criticism is saved from mere concern with technique in a literary work.

Sensibility remains, therefore, the spiritual force that vitalizes explication. Explication without an awareness of value can readily degenerate into mere concern with word meaning and structural relationships. But an awareness of the full significance of a novel's theme, for example, or of a poem's totality of meaning unites any analysis of word meanings and structural relationships with the work's inner unity and with the concentric circles of import that have this unity as their common center. Explication can then become more than a mere mechanical exercise, and, in the words of a passage from Wimsatt, "understanding and value" can advance "as far as possible in union." Would it be rash to suggest at this point that criticism in the practical sense is perhaps nothing more than the fusion in language of explicative skill and sensibility?

But does the Christian have any additional assets as a critic? In brief, what is the critical potentiality of a Christian sensibility? What can a Christian critic bring to his explication of a work of literature that a Freudian or a Marxist, for example, might lack?

The answer to such questions lies in the nature of the Christian sensibility itself. I have already stated that the Christian critic differs from other critics, if he differs at all, not so much in method as in sensibility. I have already defined "sensibility" as an awareness of values in literature. By "values" I mean that unique form of knowledge, of *la connaissance poetique,* in the language of Maritain, which literature provides as insights into the nature of man as well as into the culture created by him.

If literature is what Newman called it, namely, "the manifestation of human nature in human language," then the most comprehensive critic would be the one who would be most sensitive to all that relates to human nature in language fictively used. I suggest that a materialistic critic would be insensitive or indifferent to the spiritual values of George Herbert's "Joseph's Coat," of Gerard Manley Hopkins's "The Windhover," or Robert Lowell's "Christmas Eve Under Hooker's Statue" simply because his view of human nature is such that it excludes or tries to exclude what touches upon the spirit. I have been told that Marxist critics have already demonstrated the inflexibility of their ideology by completely ignoring the irony of Thomas More's *Utopia* and by literally interpreting the work in a vein foreign to its true meaning. If this claim is correct, then the Marxist concept of human nature has in this one regard prostituted and stunted a more comprehensive critical sensibility.

I do not mean to suggest that any Christian critic by virtue of his Christianity alone is above such a perversion, although he should be. The "club" instinct is regrettably strong. But a true Christian sensibility should never be understood to mean a sensitivity to or a preference for the work of Christians alone. The consideration by a Christian critic of the work of a Christian artist, though it may test the aesthetic distance of certain critics, does not and should not by that fact alone imply or compel critical approbation of the work. Such an assumption, rooted in a regressive nominalism, is in fact quite un-Christian and derivative of reasons or feelings that are often not even literary in nature. Martin Turnell has exposed the basic fallacy of such an approach to criticism and at the same time indicated the real nature of a religious sensibility in the tradition of Roman Catholicism:

> Thus in theory, a Catholic critic should be able to recognize valuable experience wherever he meets it and whatever the general outlook of the writer happens to be. Paradoxical though it may be, the first thing a Catholic must realize is that in the literary order dogma must never be applied dogmatically. To assume that only those experiences are valuable which are completely Christian, is to condemn oneself to sterility at the outset. They may be the most valuable experiences, but they are by no means the only valuable experiences. If we are to be true to the ideal of comprehensiveness, we must be able to sympathize with the fresh experiences that are evolved in the course of civilization. . . .

As soon as absolute truths enter the literary order, the critic who is committed to a system exposes himself to two dangers. He tends to praise works which express, or seem to express, the dogmas of his system. Thus theory perverts sensibility. . . . The other error is to condemn writers simply because their outlook is at variance with one's own system.

The true significance of the relationship between the critic and Catholicism is that the latter enriches the former, not by confining him merely to "Catholic matters" but by saving him from an erroneous or partial view of the nature of man—a nature admittedly fallen but redeemed, and, according to the enlightened, just as capable of degeneration as of glory. A less comprehensive view would tend to decrease a critic's sensitivity to these and all the concomitant values as they are presented in literature. Catholicism, with its inheritance of the classical and scholastic tradition, is capable of making a critic's sensibility more alert to the full range of man's capacity from degeneration to sanctity. Again, Turnell's words are relevant:

The advantage of a Catholic philosophy is that when properly applied it is capable of enriching the critic, of opening new horizons before him while a materialist system necessarily impoverishes him and narrows his outlook on account of its exclusiveness. A Catholic philosophy provides the most comprehensive picture of the universe; it is capable of finding a place for "all experience," particularly for those experiences which materialism is driven to explain away, to discount as abnormal or illusory because they belong to regions whose existence is incompatible with materialism.

Imbued with such a philosophy, the Catholic critic is theoretically capable of developing a sensitivity to all forms of value in literature whether they are reflective of Christian or alien traditions. Although he may dislike certain literary works or regret the paucity of literature that springs from an Incarnational concept of man or that shows "humanity . . . without its wound," in the words of Jacques Rivière, he should not for these reasons think himself spared the necessity of explicating accurately those works that reflect other or, for him, less worthy concepts of man. This is not to say that the critic's goal is disinterested appreciation. No criticism can exist permanently in a vacuum. A Catholic critic is bound to have some hierarchy of values (what else gives form to his sensibility?) and to place a greater importance on some literary works in terms of their subject matter and method of presentation. But this involves a comparative appraisal of literary worth—a relation of literary value to absolute value. Evaluation in this sense becomes more than the discernment and delineation of values in literature; it becomes assessive and capable of developing into a judgment that includes but may exceed purely aesthetic criteria. Assuming, for example, that the Catholic critic will recognize the worth of various literary experiences and avoid judging one genre by another or one age by another, he will in all probability be drawn to place a higher literary value on works in which evil is recognized by authors as more than a mere social or naturalistic aberration. Dostoyevsky's *Crime and Punishment* will in this regard probably impress him as a more valuable experience than Camus's *The Stranger,* despite the many other excellences of the latter.

However, even though a Christian sensibility will provide the framework for the formulation of such literary judgments of value, from the standpoint of critical approach and awareness alone, a Christian sensibility should enable the Christian critic to be sensitive to any work so long as it provides the perceptive reader with a "valuable experience." A "valuable experience" in literature is essentially one that provides insights into the life of man. That such insights be rooted in dogmatic truth is not necessarily a prerequisite. In literature, as in logic, it is possible to arrive at significant and worthwhile conclusions even though one's primary assumptions and premises are fallacious. Mere conformity to dogma by an author should not be a signal for a critic's approval of his work any more than a divergence from dogma should invite his immediate condemnation. This would mean that more of William Blake and possibly all of D. H. Lawrence would be unworthy of critical consideration.

Agreement and disagreement by a critic with an author's theological views or beliefs, therefore, are not the criteria for a Christian sensibility. In the practice of his art, that is, in explicating a work of literature, the Christian critic should be concerned with theological considerations primarily as they are revealed in the structural facets of a work and then only to the extent that they contribute aesthetically to the work's total meaning. This avoids the danger of considering theology as theology in literature in lieu of a proper concern with theology's aesthetic contribution to the work. Just as a critic, for example, must understand the meaning of every word in a poem as well as every allusion, symbol, or image in order to begin to understand it, so must he understand theological allusions and symbols in much the same way if his awareness to all the values in a work is to be comprehensive. It is only in this way that literary judgments as to the comparative value of a work will be, if and when the critic advances them, complete and, above all, literary.

Assuming therefore, the validity of his scholarship, and his mastery of critical "tools," I suggest that the Christian critic's first task is to imbue his explicative effort with a sensitivity to the work's values in the nondogmatic sense. He must permit his sensibility as a Christian to suffuse and direct his skill as an explicator. Such an alliance eschews the error of dogmatism, which in effect paralyzes criticism, and at the same time permits Christianity to make possible for a critic a more comprehensive approach to literature and its elucidation.

But the full significance of the relationship between Christianity and literary criticism exceeds the problems of approach and explication. Even after a critic has suspended his disbelief and entered into the life of a literary work in order to understand it as completely as possible, even though he remains faithful to his ideal of comprehensiveness and prevents his beliefs from prejudicing or dogmatizing his critical sensibility, he is still faced with the matter of evaluation. In effect, he is still confronted with the problem of relating literary value to absolute value.

Of course, the purely formalistic critic would not readily concede that relating literary value to absolute value is a matter of critical responsibility. For him, the critic's final judgments are aesthetic. But this would be a satisfactory position only if the critic were considering the literary equivalent of carpet patterns. Moreover, the nature of literature itself, to say nothing of the nature of language itself, belies the formalistic solution as complete. I make this statement in complete awareness of Herbert Read's warning that a critic should not indulge in "moral" judgments. It is important to remember in this regard that the literary work is actually a vision—indeed, a vision of the world through the very subjectivity of the artist, to paraphrase Maritain. The character of this vision, its nature as well as the skill with which it is expressed, cannot help but command the attention of the critic in an evaluative sense. Just as the beliefs of the artist condition and shape his vision of what is significant and less significant in the world, so do beliefs enter into a critic's evaluation of the vision after he has fully understood or even while he is understanding it. It not only contradicts the character of the poetic vision but also the denotative and connotative character of language to say that literature, in the language of Eliseo Vivas, is "merely formal structure devoid of embodied meanings and values." The purely formalistic solution is incomplete because it belittles the possibility of evaluating vision in any but a partial sense, and few critics have been more lucid in their castigation of this shortcoming of formalism than has Nathan Scott:

> For . . . great literature does, in point of fact, always open outward to the world, and that which keeps the universe of poetry from being hermetically sealed off from the universe of man is the poet's vision that it incarnates, of species and horizons, of cities and men, of time and eternity. This is why those modern theorists who tell us that the literary work is merely a verbal structure and that its analysis therefore involves merely a study of grammar and syntax—this is why they so completely miss the mark. They forget that writers use language with reference to what they know and feel and believe and that we can therefore understand their poems and novels only if we have some appreciation of how their beliefs have operated in enriching the meaning of the words that they employ. The "poem-in-itself," in other words, as merely a structure of language, is simply a naked abstraction, for the real poem, the real novel, is something that we can begin to appropriate only as we seek some knowledge of

the context of belief and the quality of the vision out of which it springs and with reference to which the words on the printed page have their fullest and richest meaning.

The implications of Scott's statement are that works of literature are more than interesting syntactical creations and that poems, novels, and dramas are not constructed of words as houses are constructed of so many identical and carefully positioned bricks. Thomas Pollock has stressed the same truth by saying that literature is characterized by "evocative symbolism." Springing as it does from what Maritain has perceptively called moments of "creative intuition" in the artist, a work of literature reveals a world transmuted through the artistic imagination. What results is not merely a communication, but a vision, a "verbal icon," a "concrete universal." It seems a truism to say that words have semantic as well as syntactical signification, but this is essentially what refutes the formalist. Words not only *are*. They reveal, they suggest, they mean, and in their revelation, their suggestion, and their meaning, they often project the critic beyond the realm of explication and into the domain of evaluative judgment. Richard Horchler has expressed this obvious but often ignored or slighted fact in the following statement: "Literature is an art of words, after all, and words have references outside themselves. Insofar as the literary work involves some conception of reality, viewed and valued by a human being, it must have relevance to other-than-literary views, values, and conceptions of reality." In brief, for a critic to apply only ontological or purely formalistic criteria to what springs from the deepest recesses of the spirit of man and whose significance is dependent upon the value of the "conception of reality" presented is to belittle an important dimension of artistic expression.

Archibald MacLeish concluded his famous poem, "Ars Poetica," with the now memorable line, "A poem should not mean / But be." This line could easily serve as a motto for much ontological criticism. It is a tribute to the autonomous nature of art, but as a model for all criticism it is simply inadequate. If words not only *are* but *mean* as well (as the aforementioned poem by MacLeish, for example, certainly does), then poems constituted of words not only are but mean also. In a candid article on the nature of poetic expression, William Rooney arrived at a similar conclusion by stating that a "communicative effect and an aesthetic effect are not mutually contradictory." Poems, emanating as they do from the intuition of the artist, cannot help but mean. Whatever prompted Coleridge to urge his readers to suspend disbelief in order to enter fully into the artistic experience is certainly indicative of the fact that poems in their meaning tend to raise problems of belief or disbelief, if not in the theological sense, then assuredly on the lesser level of acceptance founded on mere credulity. If works of art could not raise such problems, what would be the necessity of suspending disbelief at all even on such a basic level of response? The answer could easily be, as Walter Ong has reminded us, that the artistic experience demands the act of "belief-in," an act not of affirmation in the theological sense but of simple credulity, which is essentially Coleridge's meaning.

Such an act of "belief-in" is really, as I have already stated, the first act of critical approach. This act implies a temporary assent to but not necessarily agreement with the poet's expressed vision of the world. It is this assent or act of "belief-in" that makes the critic's experience of the poet's vision a possibility. However, the act is only preliminary to the solution of problems of greater import. After the critic has assented to and understood the poet's vision to the best of his ability, after he has made Coleridge's act of poetic faith, he may choose to exercise his critical prerogative of evaluating that vision. James Craig La Drière and Nathan Scott emphasize this need and indeed identify it as being at the very heart of the critical discipline. "The purpose of criticism," La Drière has written, "is not . . . immersion in the work, but discourse about its value; its goal is not to experience the work, but to come to terms with the experience of it in a distinct cognition which itself requires to be made intelligible in a distinct discourse." Scott has expressed this same imperative in the essay to which I have already alluded:

> For, though the literary work is a special sort of linguistic structure, that which holds the highest interest for us is the special seizure of reality toward which this structure is instrumental. It is, in other words, the nature of literature itself that compels

the critic finally to move beyond the level of verbal analysis to the level of metaphysical and theological evaluation. On this level, of course, he can establish the propriety of his judgments only by a reference to his own insights, his own scale of values, his own sense of what is important in art and in life.

It is here that the problems of evaluation come into existence, and the critic has only two possible ways of reacting to works of art in which problems at the "level of metaphysical and theological evaluation" are raised. First, he may disclaim the necessity of evaluating, as did Eliot in the early essays, saying that the art of explication or elucidation is sufficient and that the poem's value is not for the critic to determine. In other words, the critic may table the matter of evaluation and remain seemingly secure in his role of explicator or literary midwife, although even here, as Leslie Fiedler has shrewdly noted, such a critic may be guilty of self-deceit: "The 'pure' literary critic, who pretends, in the cant phrase, to stay 'inside' a work all of whose metaphors and meanings are pressing outward, is only half-aware. And half-aware, he deceives; for he cannot help smuggling unexamined moral and metaphysical judgments into his 'close analysis,' any more than the 'pure' literary historian can help bootlegging unconfessed aesthetic estimates into his chronicles." Second, one must accept the responsibility of evaluation and discharge oneself of that responsibility with all the judiciousness that it demands. However, in being judicious, the critic must be careful to avoid dogmatizing and pontification. For the Christian critic, this warning is particularly meaningful; censorial shortcuts are weak substitutes for critical thoroughness.

In effect, how and when should evaluative critical judgments be made by those who recognize evaluation as an inherent part of the act of criticism? In terms of actual practice, I contend that explication and evaluation may and perhaps should be simultaneously achieved. It is a distinct possibility and a desirable one that explication itself should be evaluative. In this I am only echoing a statement that I have already quoted from Wimsatt's "Explication as Criticism." "The extreme theory of explicative didacticism," Wimsatt has written, "cuts apart understanding and value . . . . [but] our main critical problem is always how to push both understanding and value as far as possible in union, or how to make our understanding evaluative." However, for purposes of clarity, I will consider the matter of evaluation as a postexplicative function, but the distinction should be regarded as hypothetical.

To admit that evaluation is an essential part of the act of criticism is not to say that this evaluative aspect should supplant the more pronounced modern trend of explicative criticism. It should not. In practice, explication and evaluation should be and usually are constitutive aspects of the same critical function. If it is true, as Helen Gardner has suggested, that no critic should "waste time interpreting what is not thought worth interpretation," then even the first critical contact with a literary work impels the mind toward some type of rudimentary evaluative judgment. It remains the task of subsequent critical analysis to justify or to qualify an initial evaluation of a work's quality or lack of it. The final evaluation, which in an inchoate form prompted analysis, often emerges as a vindication of an initial act of judgment corroborated by explication.

However, what problems are imposed upon a critic, particularly a Christian critic, when questions of moral or theological value are raised in a consideration of a work of literature? In other words, how should such a critic proceed to resolve the practical problems of literature and belief in arriving at an evaluative literary judgment?

This question does have an answer, although the answer is fraught with distinctions. Moreover, the answer is not one that can be reduced to mere nominalisms. I have already shown that evaluative literary judgments are possible only in an atmosphere of true catholicity, and this catholicity should be characterized by nothing less than the empathy and comprehensiveness described by Charles Moeller:

> The preliminary step in literary critique must be to set forth the whole truth as it was seen by the artist. If it is true, as Cardinal Mercier said, that every "heresy" contains a spark of truth and that this spark must be discovered, then before the work of art is run through the rolling mill of a "prefabricated system" of critique, the critic must devote all his care to the investigation

of the human datum to which the work of art bears witness. Therefore, he must "put on" the soul of its author in order to penetrate into his universe from within.

If we assume that the approach of a Christian critic is characterized by the quality described in the aforesaid passage, then what should be his criteria for evaluation? Again, a statement from Moeller's essay can serve as an excellent point of departure in arriving at an answer:

> The literary judgment proceeds rather by way of attempts to integrate partial truths into the bosom of a more comprehensive truth which is not vague and abstract but concrete because it is artistic, i.e., "incarnated." Accordingly, the order of steps to be taken by the literary critic—an order which is as necessary as it is harmonious—is: (a) to discover and express the truth of the literary masterpiece; (b) to situate it by comparing it with other works; (c) and finally to judge it by integrating it into a complete view of man.

If this philosophy and the truths that proceed from the very spirit of Christianity provide the most comprehensive picture of man, then a Christian critic's evaluative judgments of literary works would be strongly if not totally influenced by such a spirit. But here a further distinction must immediately be made. Literature is not a congeries of ideas. What is important in literature is not the idea as idea, as it is, for instance, in philosophy, but the *experience* of the idea. Rather than evaluate the idea as idea, the critic must evaluate the experience of the idea as an inherent part of his experience of the whole work. Ideational values in this sense become part of the view of man presented by the artist. It is this view of man by the artist that the critic can discuss evaluatively. This view of man must be shared and penetrated by the critic and then evaluated in relation to a vision of the whole man. The ideational values that are rife in Arthur Miller's *Death of a Salesman,* for example, must be seen not in isolation but as being interwoven into a portrait of a pathetic and, possibly, tragic human being named Willy Loman. But, in an evaluative sense, Willy Loman is pathetic or tragic because his own weaknesses and the social pressures that have aggravated them have compromised what we recognize as the inner dignity of man. Without an awareness on our part of what a man like Willy Loman should have been, could have been, or might have been (an awareness springing from our concept as critics of the nature of man), we would be at a loss to explain why his plight arouses pathetic or tragic feelings within us. Moreover, this is a spiritual and not a nominal endeavor. "If literature is the mirror of man," writes Moeller, "the critic must make this mirror shine over man in all his dimensions and keep in mind that every work of art, even if it is squarely opposed to his own personal convictions, contains fragments of humanity." Moeller adds that the critic must always be sensitive to "the presence or absence of the soul in the work, the soul in all its dimensions, as the meeting place and bridal chamber of the world here below with the world above, or the community of men with a glimpse of God."

Seeing and experiencing literature in such a way demands a sensitivity that is equally aware of the presence of truth and love in a work regardless of nominalisms that divide. In another part of this essay I said that the enlightened Christian critic is saved by Christianity from having a partial or erroneous view of man. To him, the nature of man is as capable of degeneration as of glory. He should be sensitive to the fact that these two poles establish limits between which the artist works. All that the critic should ask is that the artist's view of man remain of man and not of something more or less than man. If the critic reaches the conclusion that the artist's view of man is exaggerated or perverted or limited, the norm against which he is able to make such a statement is his vision of the whole man. In Kenneth Clark's discussion of the evaluation of the nude in art, there is a statement that is germane and analogous to this point. Clark says that "every time we criticize a figure, saying that a neck is too long, hips are too wide or breasts are too small, we are admitting, in quite concrete terms, the existence of ideal beauty." The "ideal beauty" alluded to by Clark is equivalent in a sense to a critic's view of the whole man. Unlike the beauty of the nude, which is relative and changes from generation to generation or from age to age, the view of man held by the Christian critic proceeds from the spirit of Christianity and does not fluctuate. Only a critic's finite and flawed nature or his divergences from the purifying and clarifying moments of grace can prevent his being connatured with that norm.

Actually, the norm against which the Christian critic must make his judgments is essentially the norm of charity. He cannot content himself with establishing the conventional battle lines of disagreement and hiding behind them. He must proceed to the heart of the work he is considering; he must be able to see beneath the surface of the work. Consider, for example, the incisiveness and the charitable penetration and insight of the following brief critique from an essay by Philip Scharper on such naturalistic writers as Norman Mailer, James Jones, and Nelson Algren:

> For it should be noted that most American naturalists, however illogically, have written out of a passionate moral concern which deserves our understanding and respect. If the world they picture is often sordid, there lies beneath the surface an intense conviction that it need not be, and should not be. If they show the spiritually maimed who inhabit the twilight lands of Chicago's South Side, or Schofield Barracks, or the expensive campus of a large State university, they at least do not mistake that twilight for the blaze of noon. Almost without exception the major naturalistic novels have shown in modern man the agony which feeds upon its own illusions. It is surely significant that the naturalists, in an increasingly money-conscious civilization, have repeatedly proclaimed . . . that the possession of things cannot make man happy. Obviously this is not the fullness of the gospels, but it is more congenial to the Christian than the naïve evangels of success preached all too persuasively by many contemporary educators, business men and ad-writers.

I do not single out this passage because I am in agreement with it. I think, however, that Scharper has avoided a merely nominalistic view and has tried to evaluate the view of man presented by the naturalistic writers in relation to a view of man that he thinks is truly Christian. He has seen what Moeller has called the "fragments of humanity" in the work of writers whose convictions are not the same as his own, and he has rendered an evaluation of a view of man that has emanated from artists with these convictions in a manner that strikes me as being not only sensitive and charitable but also literary.

So much for theory. Now I will attempt to examine the work of a particular poet in light of these critical principles. The poet is Wilfred Owen, and his poems are sufficiently few to allow for a relatively thorough consideration within the necessarily limited space of an essay such as this.

The fact that Owen was a soldier and wrote during World War I has tended to place an artificial stigma upon his poetry. There is something disarmingly categorical in referring to any poet as a war poet. It may imply that his poetry may have certain limitations or possibly a special dignity by virtue of the military circumstances under which it was created. Such implications often make the critical analysis and appraisal of such poetry difficult. In the case of Wilfred Owen, these implications, together with the fact, as C. Day Lewis has reminded us, that Owen, like Gerard Manley Hopkins, has been stylistically imitated by numerous admirers, have tended to obscure rather than enhance Owen's poetic merit.

It is, of course, true that Owen's best poetry was written while he was a soldier in World War I. It is also true that his experiments with assonance and "para-rhyme," as Edmund Blunden has identified it, have been extensively imitated. However, Owen's stature as a poet cannot be made narrowly dependent upon the historical event that provided the subject matter for his work (and also caused his death) nor on the post facto flattery of poetic imitation. The latter can be left as one influence for literary historians to trace, and the significance of the former has been accurately evaluated by Dylan Thomas and Vernon Watkins. "I think capital-lettered War can only in subject matter effect poetry," wrote Thomas. "Violence and suffering are all the time, and it does not matter how you are brought up against them." Similarly, Watkins has stated, "No poet is made by war, which is productive of no good. But a poet's work may be potentiated by his experience of war, and of suffering." The artistic realization of this potentiality is what must concern the critic when he turns to an analysis and evaluation of poems by a "war poet."

Despite the fact that Owen wrote that his poetry originated in the "pity of War," it is evident to any perspicacious reader of his later or "war" poems that not all spring from pity. Many of them are revelations of acrimony, protest, pessimism, outrage, and hatred. Yet Owen did write poetry that originated in the profounder well of pity. Owen, like Keats, generally acquired a more dramatic and objective voice in his poetry, a voice potentiated and purified by suffering and capable of expressing less purely personal or autobiographical responses to the war that was the source and cause of that suffering. The sensitive reader does not hear this voice in "Dulce et Decorum Est" or "The Chances," but it is at the very core of "Greater Love," "Anthem for Doomed Youth," and "Strange Meeting,"

It has been said that a man's life can frequently be understood in retrospect by regarding that life in light of its particular mission. If this has any relevance to the life of a man, it may have some relevance also to his art. In retrospect, it would appear that war was Owen's mission and his purgatory. This mission is objectified in the acrimony, protest, pessimism, outrage, hatred, and pity in Owen's poetry. Yet his passage from acrimony to pity, from the descriptive to the transfigurative, from the private to the personal cannot be chronologically traced as readily as events in a man's life. The progression from the indignation of "Dulce et Decorum Est," "Arms and the Boy," and "Smile, Smile, Smile" to the divine pity of "Miners," "Greater Love," "Anthem for Doomed Youth," and "Strange Meeting" was possibly supra-chronological, emerging in particular poems when Owen's objective correlatives were exact but otherwise remaining latent or vague when his words were not transfigurative or when the germinal idea of a poem was conceived in the heat of his own indignation rather than in his imagination.

A poem typical of indignation is "Dulce et Decorum Est." The entire series of images therein is oriented toward the Horatian motto that concludes it, *Dulce et decorum est / Pro patria mori*. In the severity of the contrast between the imagery and the motto, the poem emerges as a study in irony heightened by rhetoric. Everything in the poem seems to exist only to show the falsity of this motto in modern warfare. By indicating the "old Lie" as directly as it does, the poem becomes persuasively direct rather than imaginatively evocative. A case could possibly be made that it is more didactic than purely rhetorical, but the fact remains that the poem is essentially an outgrowth of indignation. Whatever is poetic in it is subordinated to a rhetorical end. The same could be said of the stark "S. I. W.," in which Owen comments with journalistic brevity on a soldier who, through fear, ends his own life: "With him they buried the muzzle his teeth had kissed, / and truthfully wrote the mother, 'Tim died smiling.'"

This is pessimism and disdain versified. The sequence of four poems that comprise "S. I. W." has this couplet as its fourth and concluding part, but all four parts are suffused with the same sense of disdain, which is directed toward those who see war as something it is not. Such people are symbolized in "S. I. W." by the suicide's unctuous father, who "would sooner see him dead than in disgrace," and by the mother, who would "fret" until "he got a nice safe wound to nurse." Not even the understatement and omnipresent irony in the poem can disguise its iconoclastic purpose or conceal the unmistakable influence of Siegfried Sassoon, Owen's contemporary.

Similar indignation-spawned poems are those that deal with the wounded. In these poems Owen combines an almost clinical purview with a stoic acceptance of the inevitability of such misfortune in war. Moreover, Owen frequently seems to be using the poems as an outlet for a Housman-like fatalism ("Inspection") or sardonic glee ("The Chances"). The reliance upon rhetoric is still present, and the concluding lines of the Dantesque "Mental Cases" reveal Owen's occasional propensity to lapse into a somewhat tempered didacticism:

> —Thus their hands are plucking at each other;
> Picking at the rope-knouts of their scourging,
> Snatching after us who smote them, brother,
> Pawing us who dealt them war and madness.

Yet even in this poem there is an equating of the soldier's suffering with the scourging of Christ, which is one aspect of a parallel that is at the core of Owen's best poems and that will be considered at greater length later in this essay.

In poems such as "Conscious" and "Disabled" the tone is, though free of didacticism, close to sentimentality. Both poems begin in the loneliness of unnamed soldiers alone in hospital wards and end in dismay, the dismay of men for whom there is no promising future and only a pain-ridden and almost hopeless present. It would be redundant to say that there is an inherent pathos in the circumstances of such men. After reading "Conscious" and "Disabled," one cannot help but feel that Owen has slightly battened on this poignancy. In an attempt to dramatize the plight of these wounded men, he has verged on melodrama.

To refer to these few poems as poetic failures is not to disparage much that is good in them, such as the interesting experiments with half-rhyme, translucent imagery, and the satirical implications of Owen's irony. My point is only to indicate that as organisms these poems do not wholly succeed in dramatizing poetic moments. The fault is not in the subject matter but in the poet's treatment of it. These were certainly not the poems that led Herbert Read to place Owen in "the main tradition of English poetry," a tradition including Chaucer, Shakespeare, Wordsworth, Coleridge, Browning, Hopkins, Pound, and Eliot. Nor were these the poems that prompted Dylan Thomas to say that Owen was "one of the four most profound influences on poems who came after him; the other three being Gerard Manley Hopkins, the late W. B. Yeats and T. S. Eliot." To find the Owen whom Read and Thomas have placed in such high regard, it is necessary to consider poems such as "Greater Love," "Anthem for Doomed Youth," and "Strange Meeting."

Before beginning this consideration, I must repeat a suggestion I have already made and at the same time explain that war was Owen's Passion. In my brief treatment of "Mental Cases," I noted that Owen used an image of the Passion of Christ ("scourging") as descriptive of the suffering soldiers. My reason for saying that war was Owen's Passion is not only to suggest the anonymity of "Passion" and "suffering" in the life of Owen considered as soldier but also because he himself frequently alluded to men's suffering in war as a repetition of the drama of Golgotha—an analogue to the Passion of Christ. This analogue is explicitly stated in "At a Calvary Near the Ancre":

One ever hangs where shelled roads part.
        In this war He too lost a limb,
But His disciples hide apart;
        And now the Soldiers bear with Him.

Near Golgotha strolls many a priest,
        And in their faces there is pride
That they were flesh-marked by the Beast
        By whom the gentle Christ's denied.

The scribes on all the people shove
        And bawl allegiance to the state,
But they who love the greater love
        Lay down their life; they do not hate.

This "greater love," of course, refers to the fifteenth chapter of the Gospel of Saint John: "Greater love hath no man than this, that a man lay down his life for his friends." But while "At a Calvary Near the Ancre" is the versification of this truth in an explicit way, the poem called "Greater Love" is the spontaneous unfolding and interpretation of its realization. To borrow a provocative statement by H. Coombes, there is in the latter less "a sense of formulation than of progressive creation." The "progressive creation" of "Greater Love" is structured along two motifs developed in counterpoint and culminating in the image of the Christ of the Passion in the final verse. To stress the superiority of the soldier's act of love, which can imply the necessity of sacrificing one's life for one's countrymen, to other forms of love, Owen contrasts it with sexual love. The imagery of love between man and woman, which is utilized similarly in the fifth stanza of "Apologia Pro Poemate Meo," is counterpointed with images of soldiers dead, wounded, or disfigured. "Kindness of wooed and wooer" cannot approach the soldiers' "greater love." "Red lips" are less red than the blood-stained stones on which the soldiers have fallen. The beloved's "slender attitude" does not tremble as exquisitely as bayoneted arms and legs. The beloved's voice is not as "dear" as the remembered voices of dead soldiers, nor is her hand as pale as the hands that have trailed the "cross through flame and hail."

This final image is not only a symbol of suffering but also of suffering and death accepted for the sake of others. It establishes an immediate parallel with the Passion and the Crucifixion. The soldiers' sacrifice is thus an act of immolation that hallows them and makes remote and paltry the grief of others for them: "Weep, you may weep, for you may touch them not."

This equation of the soldier's lot with Christ's lot during the Passion gives the poem a transcendental significance. The soldier is no longer pathetic in his suffering. He is exalted in his agony and ennobled while he is destroyed. "Greater Love" is thus truly elegiac in its stark and fecund simplicity, and the simplicity is the result of Owen's having found the best correlatives to express what the purifying pressures of suffering revealed to him—the "pity of war" and the poetry inherent in the pity. Despite the complexity of war and its havoc, the tone of "Greater Love" is not bitter but reverent, not negative but affirmative, not confused but translucent. "There is, in the intensity of extreme suffering," wrote John Press in an allusion to Owen, "no place for doubt or anxiety or bewilderment at the complicated nature of the modern world." This statement is certainly applicable to "Greater Love." In a moment of poetic truth and vision, Owen has accorded to human life and sacrifice the reverence that each deserves despite the distortion and mutilation imposed and inflicted by the disorder of war. In the meditative beauty of "Greater Love," the cosmos regains its perspective, and man his real dignity.

In the "Anthem for Doomed Youth," a similar counterpointing of motifs is effected in a contrast of a conventional with a military requiem, of the usual with the actual:

> What passing-bells for these who die as cattle?
>   Only the monstrous anger of the guns,
>   Only the stuttering rifles' rapid rattle
> Can patter out their hasty orisons.
> No mockeries for them; no prayers nor bells,
>   Nor any voice of mourning save the choirs,—
> The shrill, demented choirs of wailing shells;
>   And bugles calling for them from sad shires.

David Daiches's brief analysis of the imagery and contrasts in the octave is as representative as any I have read:

> The series of multiple contrasts set going between wartime life and peacetime life, between the battlefront and domestic scenes at home, by the careful choice and arrangement of images shows a grasp of poetic structure that proclaims the mature poet. The precise function in the poem of the term "cattle" (with its double suggestion of wartime horror and peacetime farming linking with similar combinations and contrasts throughout the poem), the effect of the phrase "sad shires" (with its suggestion of a denuded pastoral England sending forth its sons to die amid foreign horror) . . . are questions that could be discussed at length.

Daiches, however, ignores the significance and implications of the word "mockeries," which, if interpreted to mean travesties or burlesques, converts mere contrast into ironic contrast. Burial is usually associated with the conventional tributes of "passing-bells," "orisons," and "choirs." But the disorder of war has reversed the conventional. The usual funeral tributes mock dead soldiers for much the same reason that "English poetry," according to Owen in his memorable "Preface," "is not yet fit to speak of them." By implication, there is a certain unworthiness associated with the conventional means of tribute to the military dead. Their "bells" and "orisons" are the sounds of "guns" and rifle fire; their "choirs" are only the "wailing shells." Yet the rifle fire and the sound of shells in trajectory and upon impact are advanced as being more in keeping with the soldier' sacrifice—the final act of "greater love." The usual or conventional requiem appears in contrast as a mockery, a sham, a burlesque. This irony is mollified in the sestet, but it is the octave's sardonic quality that makes the effect of the sestet more poignant:

> What candles may be held to speed them all?
>   Not in the hands of boys, but in their eyes
> Shall shine the holy glimmers of good-byes.
>   The pallor of girls' brows shall be their pall;

Their flowers the tenderness of patient minds.
And each slow dusk a drawing-down of blinds.

Here, as in the octave, there is the contrast of the usual with the actual. The "candles," the "pall," the "flowers," the usual or conventional trappings, are contrasted with worthier forms of remembrance. The acolyte's candle is thus superseded by the glimmer of loss in the acolyte's eye, the "pall" by the "pallor of girls' brows," and the flowers by the "tenderness of patient minds" and the drawn blinds at evening. These worthier forms of remembrance suggest inward grief rather than an outward sign of loss, and this inward grief is implied as being more commensurate with the sacrifice of the "doomed youth."

"Strange Meeting" has been called by Blunden an unfinished poem, and both Daiches and Babette Deutsch consider it as such. Yet to preface a consideration of the poem with such an identification is misleading, in much the same way in which critics have been misled by regarding Coleridge's "Kubla Khan" as a fragment. Blunden does not explain where the poem seems to be unfinished; he merely notes in an appendix to his edition of the poems a number of alternative lines that Owen himself excluded.

Yet, if one regards "Strange Meeting" as a further elaboration on the theme of "greater love," then one can say that the poem is thematically entire. Like "Greater Love" and "Anthem for Doomed Youth," "Strange Meeting" is a fantasy. The Christ-like figure in the poem exceeds literal verisimilitude. He is a soldier who has been fatally bayoneted. In a "profound dull tunnel" that is reminiscent not only of a Dantesque hell but of a sepulchre, the soldier rises to confront the man who killed him. I cannot refrain from suggesting that there are Christ-like overtones even in the soldier's entombment and resurrection. However, once the scene has been established, a dialogue ensues. In response to his killer's statement that he has "no cause to mourn," the soldier who has been addressed as "Strange friend" not only expresses his regret that he has been deprived of the "undone years" but condemns the futility and hopelessness of war. Because of the propensity of men to ignore the "pity of war, the pity war distilled," the soldier prophesies that the loss of his life will probably effect no real good. As in Owen's "The Next War," there is the suggestion advanced that "greater wars" will come:

> Now men will go content with what we spoiled,
> Or, discontent, boil bloody, and be spilled.
> They will be swift with swiftness of the tigress,
> None will break ranks, though nations trek from progress.
> Courage was mine, and I had mystery,
> Wisdom was mine, and I had mastery;
> To miss the march of this retreating world
> Into vain citadels that are not walled.

Coupled with his regret and his prophetic vision is the speaker's wish that his sacrifice could have been other than in the line of a soldier's duty. If he had had a choice, he would have opted for a more ministerial form of service. It is in this wish that the analogy between the soldier and Christ is most obvious. The Christ-like character of the soldier is strengthened not only by the associative allusion to Christ at Gethsemane but also in imagery suggestive of ablution and purification:

> Then, when much blood had clogged their chariot-wheels
> I would go up and wash them from sweet wells,
> Even with truths that lie too deep for taint.
> I would have poured my spirit without stint
> But not through wounds; not on the cess of war.
> Foreheads of men have bled where no wounds were.

Without lapsing into an explicit allegory, Owen has created within a soldier's fantasy or dream of a meeting in Hell a scene that has mystical, messianic, and apocalyptic overtones. As we become spiritually attuned to the poem's theme, we are gradually prepared to accept these overtones. We recognize, in Deutsch's words, that "the figure of the man, the 'strange friend,' has grown to such significance that he is not only an allegorical image of 'the enemy' or of the spirit within each soldier that must be killed before battle can take place (the spirit of Pity) but is also the Anti-self, the conscience, the love killed by the lover, the figure of Christ." We are also prepared to accept the suitability of the half-rhymes that Owen has used to realize the poem's interwoven themes of hope and frustration, desire and disappointment. Deutsch's comment that the poem is "flawed by the obtrusiveness of the technical devices, as well as by irrelevant archaisms" is made in complete disregard of the fact that the effect of half-rhyme is diatonic and, therefore, uniquely suited to the disharmony and cacophony of war and the interwoven themes of the poem—"the bitter frustration by war of the ecstatic creativity of the human spirit." Finally, we realize that "Strange Meeting" develops the mystical aspect of the Christ-soldier analogy. The soldier who speaks in this poem is one who has suffered the Passion out of "greater love" and who has not *made* but *been* the sacrifice. He has passed beyond death's dominion. Yet his legacy, even for the man who killed him, is forgiveness:

> I am the enemy you killed, my friend.
> I knew you in this dark; for so you frowned
> Yesterday through me as you jabbed and killed.
> I parried; but my hands were loath and cold.
> Let us sleep now. . . .

One hears in "Strange Meeting" as well as in "Anthem for Doomed Youth" and "Greater Love" the dramatic voice of Wilfred Owen. Freed of the influences of Keats and Sassoon and purified by suffering, Owen was able to articulate "the pity war distilled." Yet, to call him a war poet, as we must in the historical sense, does not mean that we should ignore or belittle those elements in his best poems that transcend military bounds. The basis for the transcendence is Owen's equation of the soldier's suffering and death with the Passion and death of Christ. Owen, with thousands of others, underwent this Passion. As a soldier, he saw "God through mud" and shared in a twentieth-century counterpart of Golgotha the "eternal reciprocity of tears." In his best poems, which are his testament, he has transfigured rather than mirrored this experience and left a dramatization of the meaning of suffering in war, whose transcendental significance is central to a complete understanding of his art.

How can any writer reach fixed conclusions on a subject so fraught with the need to make accurate distinctions in thousands of particular instances where the problem of literature and belief is raised? Indeed, a conclusion might suggest that the problem has been solved, when actually it is a problem that must be solved as often as it is confronted. At best, I have only synthesized and advanced a few suggestions that could be adapted toward the problem's timelessness and have tried to show their applicability to the work of a particular poet, Wilfred Owen. But the problem must be faced and considered, and it must be faced and considered in terms of the present. As La Drière has warned, "Criticism is judgment, not a memory of judgment, still less the reconstruction of a judgment that might have occurred, or of one that did occur in the past." To avoid or shirk the need for making literary judgments amounts to a denial of the problem, and to deny the problem for whatever reason is to deny criticism not only its contemporaneity but also a good deal of its value.

II

Endthoughts of a Recent Retiree

A decade ago I retired from teaching at Duquesne University, where I had worked most of my adult life. There was no single compelling reason. I had the opportunity to retire more than five years earlier but decided not to because I quite frankly enjoyed working with students. Five years later the decision seemed to make itself, and I wrote my official letter of resignation, cleaned out my office, turned in my office key, and, like Longfellow's Arabs, proceeded to "silently steal away."

For some reason I thought that leaving the university would actually simplify my life. It was not too long before I discovered how wrong I was. First, the retirement plan that I thought was already decided became a matter of alternatives. Each prospective plan seemed more attractive than the other, but it required the know-how of a corporate attorney to understand both the large and small print. Eventually, I relied on the authority of a friend in the office of Faculty Benefits to point me in the right direction. That done, I woke to a series of incessant and gratuitous telephone solicitations. One caller wanted to know if I was interested in the latest hearing aids. Another asked if I had thought of joining the American Association of Retired Persons. Concurrent with these calls was an abundance of incoming mail, also gratuitous, also incessant. One letter informed me that I was now eligible for Security Blue; another said that I would do better with a Security Blue alternative. A letter from a doctor of unknown repute asked me if I was aware of a sudden drop in testosterone. The Sinclair Institute sent me a booklet so that I could order videos that demonstrated that there indeed was sex after fifty, a fact that I had no reason to question either personally or otherwise. One solicitor asked me whether liver spots were beginning to appear on my skin. Finally, I received a telephone call from a rather pleasant woman who wanted to know if I had already purchased a grave site. If not, she said, it was now possible for a limited time to purchase two for the price of one, but I had to buy it (I am not making this up) before I died. I told her to mail me the information, which, of course, she did. I am expecting a follow-up call at any moment.

While dealing with all of these new designs upon my life, I began to wonder when I ever had had time to work. Then it became apparent to me that there must be some central computerized data bank that lists senior citizens, and once you are on the list, you are fair game. It was not far different from the other unsolicited letters in which I was informed that I might "already be the winner" of an astronomical amount of money to be factored down to controllable six-figure deferred sums made payable to me forever. In other words, being retired simply meant that I had become a different kind of target, but a target nonetheless.

With my life no longer semestered into segments, I found that I was able to develop a more balanced perspective regarding my profession and how it had changed and been changed. I had long since accepted in spirit and letter the implications of a memorial statement by A. Bartlett Giamatti that "the heart of the university is liberal education, and the heart of liberal education is the art of teaching." In recent decades I had reluctantly come to accept the existence of the increasing number of deconstructionists, militant feminists, and other "ists" whom the graduate schools were certifying as college teachers but who were not really interested in teaching at all. Research was their forte, and invariably it was research into obscure authors whose work was suddenly made to seem important for reasons that had nothing to do with literary value. Doctoral theses were written about this tribe of the "undeservedly neglected." Such theses were the creations, not of literary critics, but of theorists or, more frequently than not, ideologues. All too often they had no real knowledge of the literature of their profession. A colleague of mine asked one of them once if she had read much of John Milton. Her answer was that she had not because she was still involved with "structuralism."

Being out of the profession on a day-to-day basis permitted me to see that this was not a local but a national (even an international) phenomenon. I learned from casual research that such deconstructionist saints as Derrida and Foucault were never really taken seriously by the French and were finally regarded almost as jokes, even though American graduate schools took them to their collective bosoms. Small wonder, then, that the number of undergraduates majoring in literature or history or other solids today is continuing to decline if their classes are taught by theorists whose knowledge of the solids in their respective disciplines is almost nil. Moreover, if a tradition of humanism is vanishing from graduate education, then how will it be possible for various ongoing perversions of literary and other studies to be counteracted, let alone corrected, in times to come?

Concurrent with such degeneration in liberal studies, there now exists the problem of tailoring education to student desires, which is nothing more than regarding students as customers for whom an "educational product" must be designed. Hence, the creation of courses that are purely vocational. The role of liberally educated teachers (those who still exist) in this schema is to service the vocational programs, nothing more. The administrators who are behind this adulteration of education are invariably not educators at all. They see themselves as managers; and, frankly, what can be expected of managers except managerial, not educational, decisions?

Catering to the short-term interests of students is nothing new. Fly-by-night schools have been doing it for years. What's new is that the fly-by-night philosophy has been adopted by many universities and colleges. Granted, many undergraduates are concerned with what they will do upon graduation, particularly if they have incurred tuition debts to be repaid after they receive their degrees. Granted, this might tend to influence their educational undergraduate choices. But acquiring the skills of doing has always been secondary to the acquisition of the skills of being, as every true educator understands. The skills of doing equip students for a particular job, even if it's a job that may be here today but gone tomorrow. The skills of being have as their goal the readying of a student for whatever comes, which is a much more comprehensive as well as realistic ideal, since it's well known that most people in their lifetimes change "jobs" three or four times. Awakening students to the importance of the skills of being is what liberal education strives to do. When I discussed this once with a corporate recruiter, he said succinctly, "What good is a liberal education anyway? All it teaches you to do is think."

I came to see that in matters of education and in many other facets of modern life there was missing not only a sense of hierarchy and value but also one of simple proportion. In many colleges and universities the most frequently cited example is the disproportionate importance placed upon intercollegiate athletics and the athletes involved in them. The real problem here is not simply what many have already noted, namely, the schmoozing of prospective stars by coaches and alumni, the big money associated with the various bowls, the creation of special courses (with tutors) for those who are athletically gifted but not intellectually qualified to survive a standard college curriculum. The real problem is the mania for victory—victory at all costs. Perhaps this is due to the fact that we Americans are a people who can't *not* win. When translated into the pressures this hunger creates in college athletics, the results are stupefying. Coaches are lionized; a former coach at the University of Alabama was once nominated for the presidency of the United States. Some intercollegiate rivalries become miniwars. Braggadocio reigns on the playing field. And all this is justified as a form of character building. Robert Maynard Hutchins, after excising football from the University of Chicago when he was named its chancellor, was criticized by vociferous alumni and others for eliminating an activity that they regarded as essential to the development of character in the life of "student athletes." Hutchins's reply was that there was as much a connection between football and character formation as there was between bullfighting and agriculture. But leaving aside the acerbic, a case actually could be made that character is strengthened more by a person's response to defeat rather than to the hubris of victory since men often confront their true stature only after tasting defeat in college athletics or, for that matter, in anything, including, for example, the Vietnam War.

Disproportion appears in other ways as well. College and university presidents act and are often paid like CEOs. Six-figure salaries are common here, and the gap between such administrators and the salaries of even the highest-ranking professors is formidable. In the same context we are confronted with the spectacle of part-time or adjunct teachers who are paid Mexico's wages on an hourly scale — between $800 and $2,500 per credit hour per semester (these figures are approximations of the national average) with no fringe benefits at all. Then there is this reflection of what passes for a just wage in the corporate world, where CEOs are richly compensated while those in the workforce who created the profits for the company are treated penuriously or fired in the name of downsizing or rightsizing or some other euphemism. In my city the CEO of a major bank receives more than a million dollars a year while one college graduate was hired at the same bank for a starting salary of $12,000.

One of the most egregious forms of disproportion is caused by our mischievous inclination to canonize entertainment as a sine qua non of social life. I do not mean to limit entertainment to everything from theater to nightclub acts to whatever fun can be taken to mean. I mean sports as entertainment, education as entertainment, print journalism and television news as entertainment, religion as entertainment, travel as entertainment, and so on. Like Ex-Lax, everything is somehow supposed to taste good no matter what its real purpose and nature are. The consequences of this lunacy for education are degenerative, to say the least. Witness the scourge of phonics instead of traditionally taught spelling as but one example. In matters of religion, witness the various televised revivalist orators who make Elmer Gantry seem like a piker. In matters of communications, witness the musical and electronically enhanced openings of the evening news on any of the major networks, proving nightly that Paddy Chayefsky was right about news as theater where calamity can be presented as diversion.

All of these shortcuts and inequities contribute to the ongoing burgeoning of disproportion in our entire national life. It manifests itself in our cult of personality. Audiences pay millions of dollars to see a convicted rapist and flesh-eater return to the heavyweight division. A president's pettifoggery under oath about fondling an all-too-willing female intern is seen by some as high treason. It's also all too obvious even in our uneven scale of memorialization. In Washington, for example, a capacious park and garden memorialize Lyndon Johnson and Lady Bird. Ronald Reagan's recently opened palace in the same city rivals in square footage the Pentagon, while President Roosevelt's self-requested memorial is but a stone slab no larger than the size of his desk. John F. Kennedy, his widow, his two children, and his brothers occupy a single plot in Arlington. Beside the Potomac the names of 58,000 futile deaths alphabetized on a black marble wall displace barely an acre.

Realistically speaking, what's so new about disproportion? Has it not always been so? The traditional response of the idealistic young is to restore proportion to the world, to change what *is* into what *ought to be,* to convert envisioned possibilities into facts. Having recently entered the official ranks of senior citizenry and being now a prospective member of the American Association of Retired Persons, I feel no less idealistic than I felt when I was twenty-five. The only difference is that my expectations are more modest. I have long since accepted the contention of Camus that we live within limits, that our efforts are all too often tempered by limits, and that the results of our efforts can never be guaranteed in advance. As T. S. Eliot has noted in this regard, "For us there is only the trying."

Living as I do in a city (Pittsburgh, Pennsylvania) and county (Allegheny) that have the second-highest percentage of senior citizens in the entire country, I am surrounded by many people my age and older. They seem to be rooted and resilient. I have never seen in Pittsburgh what I observed once in St. Petersburg, Florida, namely, a device for taking one's own blood pressure free of charge at the entrance of more than one drug store. If old age is what Thomas More called it—"the best part of our lives and the most discreet"— then I think that my fellow citizens would assent to the discretionary part of that statement. Many others would find more in common with E. B. White's response when he was asked what it was like to be seventy. He said that it was not much different from being forty or fifty except that he woke up at least once every night to go to the bathroom. White was asked no further questions.

Provence of the Six Winds

To learn to do it. To compact into a specific number of words what
Smollett, Stendhal, Ford Madox Ford, Henry James, M. F. K. Fisher,
Marcel Pagnol, Michael Jacobs, Lawrence Durrell, and, most recently and profitably, Peter Mayle needed whole books to do. To re-
create the tennis-audience look of sunflowers near Avignon as they
follow the daily lob of the sun in uniform obedience. To describe the
rinsed and detail-enhancing light that, according to legend, permitted Don Quixote to regain his sanity when he returned to the Spanish equivalent of these latitudes and that later attracted Van Gogh,
Bonnard, Renoir, Matisse, and Picasso. To leave off reading the entablature on the great door of St. Gilles and drive past the grazing
fields where the surly black bulls of the Camargue stand and stare
like sculpture. To invoke the salad of scents that are yours for the in-
haling: jasmine and lavender, croissants at dawn, the seawinds from
the Mediterranean, the primal fertility odors in camembert and brie.
To pause at St.-Laurent-du-Var and remember as you look seaward
that Antoine de Saint-Exupéry vanished without a trace in his Lockheed Lightning south of this coast in 1944. To confront the Pont du
Gard for the first time and wonder how few people know the name
of M. Vipsanius Agrippa, the architect who designed the arched two-
storied bridge of beige rock. To feel the presence of the past be-

neath your soles as you negotiate the cobbled, drain-divided streets of Gourdon, Eze, Tourettes-sur-Loup, St. Paul de Vence, and other *villages perchés*. To be in Uzès on market day and see how the alphabet of colors in bolts of Provençal fabric actually outdoes the natural tints in lemons, eggplants, scallions, tuna, shrimp, corded thighs of lamb, and the dull maroon of wet liver. To contrast the latent hedonism you see here with the knowledge that Avignon was the home of seven popes (not all exemplary in a city that shocked Petrarch) and that cloisters, shrines, and abbeys are plentiful in a country that has always regarded itself as the oldest daughter of the Roman Catholic Church. To learn that a monastery founded by Saint Honoratus on the Iles de Lérins off the coast of Cannes provided Europe with more than nine hundred bishops and that one of them went to a certain fame in Ireland. To the consternation of all who believe otherwise, a plaque on the wall of the still-functioning monastery proclaims that Saint Patrick was one of the nine hundred.

All of these descriptive challenges await me as I zoom south from Paris to Avignon on the TGV (Train à Grande Vitesse, or high-speed train), forgoing a jet arrival in Nice. After receiving much advice about "how to write about Provence," I have decided that I will proceed like a whale swimming through clouds of plankton, swallowing indiscriminately, digesting selectively. Or I will imitate Diogenes by going wherever curiosity dictates. I will look, listen, taste, touch, and smell. I will appreciate the contrasts.

Outside the speeding windows of the TGV pass stationary herds of the beef cattle of Burgundy, nuclear power plants, pruned vineyards on terraced hillsides bordering the parallel Rhône (probably a corruption of Rhodes from the time when the first Greeks came to Provence in 600 BC), then the soupy warmth of Avignon in July. From the France of Paris to the France of Avignon is an experience in decompression as if the passage is not from one latitude to another but from one culture to another, and, in a sense, it is. In a frequently quoted statement, Victor Hugo implied as much when he wrote: "In France, one argues; in Avignon, one kills." It was as if he were speaking of another country.

Ahead of me is a month's tour of Provence, but first I have to deal with Jean-Luc of Avis. I show him my auto rental papers and ask him in French if he speaks English. "A lee-tle," he answers. This is the French's classic way of avoiding the need to respond to difficult questions by pretending that they know less than they know. Jean-Luc studies the papers and begins "explaining me" that my reservation cannot be for the Saab I have been promised since he has no Saabs. He will find an alternative.

"Is the car air-conditioned? Not ventilated, but air-conditioned?" I ask. I've been to the south of France in July before, and I know what it means to boil behind the wheel.

"But of course," he says, as if I've raised a question of honor.

"Are you sure?"

"But of course."

Prior to my dealing with Jean-Luc, I listened to a strident conversation between his associate and two Americans arguing in Long Island English about a car that the associate could not produce.

"Here's the paperwork guaranteeing the car," said the first American.

"Guaranteeing," stressed the second American.

"But I do not have the car," said the associate, using the French tactic of becoming icily correct when pressed—not annoyed, just correct. "If Monsieurs will be patient, I will make a research."

"We're not leaving here without a car," said the first American.

"If Monsieurs will be patient."

While the associate "researched" at his computer, the Americans sulked, huffed, and spoke in vicious whispers about Franco-American relations.

"Would Monsieurs accept a larger car in the next higher category at the same rate?" asked the associate calmly.

End of controversy. The Americans left happy. Franco-American protocols had been repaired. The associate had done what the French do to perfection—reward after delay. Jean-Luc repeats this procedure with me. I forget my Saab and drive off in a freshly washed Ford Mondeo with only 2,000 kilometers on the odometer.

Looking for the correct entry gate into the walled city of Avignon, I pass directional signs for Arles, Nîmes, Aix-en-Provence, and Tarascon. The French excel at this kind of road signage, and I feel reassured that I will always be able to find my way to these and other destinations in the weeks ahead. But driving into Avignon was a different story. I had never driven into a walled city before. Inside the walls, I felt that I was behind the dikes that were holding out the soiled seas of this world. I edged forward slowly behind the behinds of pedestrians to whom my car was totally irrelevant. The streets that led to my hotel seemed made for carts rather than cars. At one point I actually brushed the mirror on the passenger side against an open door. I would have similar experiences later in Haut-de-Cagnes and Roussillon where clearances had to be gauged in fractions of inches.

Finally, the Hotel Mirande. It was literally in the very shadow of the Palace of the Popes. On the days that followed, I strolled the sloped plaza (the size of a soccer field) that separated the palace from the Institute of Drama opposite where Gérard Philipe served his apprenticeship. Tourists aimed their cameras or video recorders at the austere walls of the palace, at the strategically placed Botero sculptures on the plaza itself, at the organ-grinder (a boy of, perhaps, ten) who cranked out Provençal folksongs while his terrier snoozed obliviously on top of the grinder itself.

But where and what is Provence? Marine Bruel, a graphic artist from Boston but reared in the Var and the Vaucluse where her mother still lives, says, "Provence is a feeling." For her, the feeling should include Nîmes and Uzès and other places in the Gar and Languedoc. When I demur and point to a map delineating the five departments of Provence as the Bouches-du-Rhône, Vaucluse, Var, Hautes-Alpes, and Alpes-Maritimes, she says definitively, "Geographers are not historians." Her view is echoed by James Pope-Hennessy, among others: "The whole area of Provence from the Maritime Alps to the Rhône, from the Dauphiné to the sea, is made homogenous by the universal culture of the olive and the vine, by the language, traditions, ideas and physique of the people who inhabit it. . . . . Though technically in the Languedoc, Nîmes and the Pont du Gard belong by cultural tradition to Provence." Such floating definitions are not uncommon. The drawn contours of Provence on the cover of the Michelin Guide, for example, delineate the boundaries to include Nîmes in the east, Aix-en-Provence in the west, Lyons in the north, and Marseilles in the south.

And what of the Riviera? The cartographers include Nice, but one Frenchman tells me pejoratively, "Nice is not Provence. Nice was not even a part of France until the last half of the nineteenth century. Nice was Savoy—Italian." The problem is made no simpler by authors. The novels of the great Provençal author Jean Giono suggest that Provence for him was the area around his home village of Manosque. Then there is Ford Madox Ford, who loved Provence to the extent that he claimed "if we except Periclean Athens, [Provence] is the only real civilization that the world has yet seen." Nonetheless, he contends that everything west of the Rhône is not Provence, adding that Provence "is not a country nor the home of a race, but a frame of mind." Well, how does one frame a frame of mind? Finally, there are those who say that Provence begins at the Mediterranean and ends at the "olive line," the line above which olive trees do not grow. Where do these often conflicting definitions leave me? Better to begin with the France of the cartographers but to leave room for poetic license, which permits Provence to be a feeling or an idea without boundaries. If contradicted, I will give a Cartesian shrug and say, "Provence is Provence."

"Provence has been inhabited since the Stone Age," wrote Bérenger-Féraud, the retired naval physician who named the five departments in 1885. Etchings in the Valley of Merveilles alone would seem to substantiate this. But France's significant demographic history begins in the tenth century BC with the Ligurians. Four hundred years later the Greeks arrive, colonizing and developing Marseilles (Massilia) as well as La Ciotat (Kitharista), Hyères (Albia), Antibes (Antipolis), St. Tropez (Athenopolis), Nice (Nikaia), and Monaco (Monoikos). They in turn are followed by the Celts (Arles originates from the Celtic Ar-lath) and the maritime Arabs of the Levant whom the Greeks called Phoenicians. Then came the Romans, whose imprint on Provence (Provincia Romana and Gallia Narbonensis) is the most definitive of all. Intermingle subsequent incursions by Teutons, Vandals, Saracens, and Visigoths. Accelerate the centuries of migration, resettlement, invasion, and intermarriage, then include 250,000 *pieds noirs* (French colonials) and *harkis* (pro-French Algerians) as well as Tunisians and Moroccans, and you end with a population mix of blood and cultures that can only be called Mediterranean.

Apart from demographics, what manifests itself constantly in Provence is the imposition of a Christian culture upon a pagan one, with the former using the latter for its own enrichment and purposes whenever necessary. I sense this when I visit the deservedly famous Roman theater in Orange, an acoustical marvel backed by the mother of all walls. When I leave, I notice the small chapel of St. Florent in the very shadow of the amphitheater. An accidental or deliberate proximity? If deliberate, why? I will see the same pattern in Arles where the cloisters and chapel of Ste. Trophime are adjacent to the coliseum-like theater. But nowhere is this more striking than at the Alyscamps in Arles. The parallel columns of stone sarcophagi lead to the church of St. Césaire at the end. Was there some need to raise a Christian structure in order to "baptize" the pagan one by having it positioned in the immediate vicinity?

When I mention these proximities of pagan and Christian sites to John Templeton, a retired British admiral who has lived in Provence for more than a quarter of a century, he says, "Why not? Christmas and Easter, after all, are built on pagan feasts. Here the physical evidence of the same tendency is all around us." As he speaks, a Mirage fighter jet, practicing a subradar maneuver known as contour flying, streaks overhead like a burst of summer thunder, reminding everyone that the feast of war changes only in means, not intent. "Actually the people here are more influenced by the weather than by pagan or Christian finalities. Our weather is like that fighter that just passed. It changes sensibilities. When it's marvelous, it's more marvelous than anywhere else, but it's as bad as anywhere when it's bad. Look at what happened in Vaison-la-Romaine. Storms and a flood. The Provençaux are like that. When they're kind, they're kinder than anyone. But there's an underlying violence. Sometimes it just bursts out. Like the mistral. Like the wind." As I listen, I recall the famous three curses of Provence: taxes, the river Durance, and the mistral. I cannot help but note how two of the three have to do with nature, which makes me take Templeton's theory seriously.

Later, when I look down from the ash-white peak of Mont Ventoux or the rust-colored ramparts of Roussillon on what Shakespeare's Duke of Burgundy described as "our fertile France," I am overwhelmed by the mix of utility and beauty. The land is plotted for maximum yield. The rock gorges, crevasses, mini-Alps, and the impenetrable maquis in the valleys and foothills give way to flawlessly neat farms and vineyards. (What did Petrarch see when he climbed Mont Ventoux in 1336, supposedly the first man to do it?) On the same day I drive to Les Baux. I see the same contrast—the fertility of the flatlands (interrupted by cooperatives where the grape farmers truck their harvests for processing) and the rock ledges and monoliths where Les Baux of the troubadours perches. Fertility and severity: are these the two poles on which the world of Provence turns?

Somehow the combination of geography, climate, manners, work, and temperament have created a seasonal inclination in the Provençaux to celebrate. From Nîmes to Menton, from Sisteron to Ste. Maxime there are festivals, festivals, festivals. There are festivals for mimosa, jasmine, roses, films, jazz, saints, harvests, feast days, celebrities (a Gérard Philipe film festival, for example, in Ramatuelle where Philipe is buried), horses in Stes. Maries de la Mer, pottery, wine, poetry (the International Contemporary Poetry Meeting in Tarascon), lemons (the lemons used in the parade floats in Menton are subsequently crushed, boiled into marmalade, and bottled for the attendees), accordions, chestnuts, silence (only the French would think of this in the same way as only the French would headline "Mort d'un Poète" when Léo Ferré died in the summer of 1993 and relegate the difficulties of the franc to a position of lesser importance on the front page of *Nice Matin*), and, finally and gloriously, humor (in Aubagne).

Common also in Provence is the interchangeability of fact and legend. Facts often become legends, and legends facts. Whether Mary Magdalene, Mary Salome, and the sister of the Virgin Mary ever sailed to the spot so marked at Stes. Maries de la Mer is too immersed in myth to confirm, but the cult of the three Marys exists in the minds of the population as a historical certainty. Add this to the area's history and sociology, and you have a mixture within a mixture within a mixture. Imagine going to a summer Sunday bullfight in the Roman Coliseum in Nîmes where Spanish toreros perform before a crowd that is defiantly bourgeois, predominantly Protestant, and descended from the Huguenots, who successfully resisted the

French king in a squabble over the Albigensian heresy. If that's not a potpourri, what is?

Compound this by including the recent influx of Algerians, Tunisians, Moroccans, and other North Africans who are bringing Islam with them into a country that is nominally Catholic. This has even provoked debate about transforming France's traditional orientation so that it will accommodate two religions. Actually, this is the inevitable fruit of French imperialism in North Africa and elsewhere— a colonialism in reverse. The problem will not go away. What is sown will be reaped even if the sowing and the reaping are the lots of different generations. If this reaches a point in France where Islamic fundamentalism is pitted against French chauvinism, the consequences could be ugly indeed. Chauvinistic or not, the French have no intention of permitting their culture to be adulterated by immigrants who do not integrate. Ironically, however, their latent prejudice against the North Africans does not invite integration as much as it encourages tribalism. What results is suspicion, discord, and violence. In parts of Marseilles such as La Cayolle, fights between the police and unemployed North African youths are not uncommon. Such incidents feed the racist appeals of Jean-Marie Le Pen's National Front. It even inspired Valéry Giscard d'Estaing, during his presidency, to urge that French citizenship should be determined by French parentage and not merely by proof of birth on French soil—citizenship by womb. This blatantly biological qualification may have been prompted by fear of numbers. Today, half of France's four million immigrants are North African or from Arab countries. This has prompted the government to attempt to reduce future immigration to zero, even though it is openly acknowledged that 100,000 illegal immigrants enter the country annually from North Africa alone. How does one reconcile immigration with national needs, human rights, and constitutional principles? This problem will challenge intelligent and cultural leaders for decades to come. In this regard, the responses of Le Pen, who is now a power in Nice as well as in Marseilles, and of d'Estaing seem reactionary at best.

Putting aside for the moment the problems of immigration and integration, it is hardly surprising that Provence is attractive to outsiders. The geography, the climate, the agriculture, and the way of life are inducements in themselves. In addition, the Christianity of the south is less Jansenistic and Cartesian than it is in the north. It is more of the blood, more suited to the senses, more "of this world." For these and other reasons people have come here as invaders, traders, conquerors, visitors, immigrants, transplanted residents, or tourists. The list is a long one and includes Celts and Berbers as readily as the floating royalty of Russia, Nijinsky, Gerald and Sara Murphy, Cole Porter, Ernest Hemingway (who expanded a short story called "Mr. and Mrs. Eliot" into a posthumously published novel called *The Garden of Eden,* centering it in La Napoule), W. Somerset Maugham (who treated Spencer Tracy with hauteur when they were introduced in Cap Ferrat), Van Gogh, Dirk Bogarde for a brief time, Stephen Spender, "Baby Doc" Duvalier (whom I saw lounging languidly with his retinue on the beach in Cannes and lunching on champagne and ice cream), Lebanese who have relocated here since the war, Peter Mayle (whose *A Year in Provence* and *Toujours Provence* are in every bookstore in the area in trade and deluxe editions), Albert Camus, Yves Montand, Jeanne Moreau, Brigitte Bardot, Isadora Duncan (who was strangled on the Boulevard des Anglais in Nice when her scarf became entangled in the wheel of the sports car in which she was a passenger), Sartre, Saint-Exupéry (who retreated to Le Cagnard in Haut-de-Cagnes for seclusion), Spencer Tracy (who loathed W. Somerset Maugham before and after he met him), a Saudi Arabian prince whose unique car was designed to resemble a camel, assorted English men and women following in the footsteps of Queen Victoria and settling in Cimiez and Grasse. The list is endless.

Regardless of what attracted such a diverse population to Provence, the fact remains that Provence is a part of the world to which people come (however temporarily) rather than from which people go (however temporarily). Ford Madox Ford attributes much of this to spices and the enhancing and seducing effect these have on the cuisine that people want to eat here. "Provence is the only country in the world," he writes, "to contain a sufficiency of spices." Provence is a veritable spicery with its native "mint, thyme, tarragon, verjuice, verbena, fennel, lime-flowers, bitter-oranges, lemons, absinthe . . . olives, basil, garlic . . . pimento . . . peppers and mustard." Ford then notes that more wars have been fought over spices than over religion but that the Provençaux, though involved in many battles with invaders, "only once in recorded history issued from their borders in an aggressive war." His conclusion is that "Provençal digestions are tranquilized and her populations content to stay at home."

In this sense, Provence (contradicting Hemingway's view of Paris) is not "a moveable feast." People must come to Provence to share and experience it. Or to dream of it longingly and praise it in poetry and song. When Keats had intimations of death in England after hearing the song of a nightingale, he longed "for a draught of vintage! that hath been / Cool'd a long age in the deep-delved earth, / Tasting of Flora and the country green, / Dance, and Pro- vençal song, and sunburnt mirth." Peire Vidal, one of Provence's greatest poets, wrote of it as one would write of a beloved parent or mentor: "I drink deep into my lungs wind that I know comes from Provence; / From that country everything that comes gives me plea- sure / And listening to the praises of her I smile. / For every word of praise that is said I ask for a hundred / So much I am pleased by the praise of that land. / From the mouth of the Rhône to Valence, between the sea and Durance! / In that noble land did I leave the joy of my heart. / To her I owe the glory that the beauty of my verses and valor of my deeds have gained for me, / And as from her I draw talent and wisdom, so it is she that made me a lover and, if I am a poet / To her I owe it."

There are countless other tributes by poets, from Frédéric Mis- tral to Yves Bonnefoy. Mistral, who won the Nobel Prize for Litera- ture in 1904, not only praised Provence in his poems but even went so far as to donate all of the Nobel money to perpetuate Provençal letters and culture through the Arlaten Museum in Arles. Bonnefoy, who lived in Provence before accepting a post in Boston, wrote nos- talgically about his life there for years afterward. And René Char of- fers this simple, defining tribute in *Leaves of Hypnos*: "This rock-hold of fine people is a citadel of friendship. Everything that blurs lucidity and hampers confidence is banished from this place. We have been wedded once and for all in the presence of the essential."

I discuss this symbiosis of literature and landscape during a meeting with Anne Wade Minkowski in her remodeled farmhouse in Les Astéries in the Vaucluse. An Arabist and translator (of the poetry of Adonis, a perennial Nobel candidate), she says, "The influence of the Andalusian Arabs on Provence is considerable. It's quite subtle, however, and it's not frequently acknowledged."

Later I discuss this influence with Ian Meadows, a Scot living in Saint-Julien-de-Briola near Carcassonne and an authority on the Arabs in Occitania. "The origins of the Parsifal legend and that of the Holy Grail come from southern France," Meadows tells me. "Also it's the mother of lyric poetry in the West. It's not only what made Petrarch Petrarch but also what inspired Dante to make Beatrice a symbol for sanctifying grace in *The Divine Comedy.* Shakespeare's *Romeo and Juliet,* Donne's love lyrics, and even Herrick's poems are in the same tradition. The prototypes of Western love originate in Provence as well."

The tradition to which Meadows refers begins with the troubadours, who are the bridge between Andalusian Arab Spain and Provence. The word "troubadour" itself is derived from the Arabic *al-tarab,* which can be roughly translated as a state or mood evoked by beautiful music. The musical poems of the troubadours had as their subject the praise of a beautiful but unattainable woman. This tradition can be traced to Sufism, with the woman being addressed as if she were divine, a substitute for God. As man's love for God is unrequitable in life, so is the lover's for his beloved.

What the Andalusian Arabs and the troubadours created was a poetry of perpetual desire as opposed to a poetry that stressed gratification. "The longing of the troubadour, always unsatisfied and never exhausted," Giovanna Magi has written, "is the centre of the whole new conception of poetry and love." In brief, Raimbaut d'Orange, Folquet de Marseille, Peire Vidal, and other troubadours made poetry and music out of romantic anguish.

When this tradition of the troubadours collided with the poetic tradition of Rome in Provence, which could and did accommodate ribaldry, vulgarity, and the copulatory poems of Catullus, the offspring created the schizophrenic basis for courtly love and subsequently for Western love in general. The sung praises of the unattainable and divinized woman—an impossibility in fact—created for a time and possibly for all time the image of a dream-woman. The lover inevitably searched for her in a person other than his wife, she being reserved for bearing and rearing children and household management, a Catullan *hausfrau*. Of course, one could never marry the dream-woman under the codes of courtly love since that would make the dream real, and one could not know in advance if the love was transferable. As Denis de Rougemont has written, the result is the ongoing split between passion and conjugal love, between romance and marriage. Observe grand opera or soap opera, and there it is. The element of romance is often not integrated or transformed into the dailiness of married life. This compels either mate in a tired or routinized marriage to believe that romance with all its attractiveness, its excitements, its uncertainties, and its superficial nobility is by definition extramarital. Hence, "affairs," "the other woman," "mistresses," et cetera. The Arabs and troubadours at least had the good sense to believe that romantic love should be unrequited. They knew that reality and satiety were its natural enemies. Better to sing of it than live it.

Ian Meadows documents parallels between the Arab poems of romantic suffering and many of Provençal origin. He notes, for example, that Peire Vidal's search for the wild she-wolf of the Pennautier is directly derivative of Ibn Zaldun's for the daughter of the caliph of Mustakfi in the eleventh century. This in turn is linked to the other Arab legend of the mad lover (Majnun) who searched the desert endlessly for his beloved Leila. It also has affinities with the Celtic persona of Aengus. In William Butler Yeats's "Song of Wandering Aengus," Aengus pursues "a glimmering girl" until he is "old with wandering." Is the connection far-fetched? Not necessarily, if you recall that the Celts were long a part of Provence and that Yeats himself, in play and poem, was aware of the Arab influence upon them.

Just as the troubadours transformed the legacy of Arab Andalusia into a language and melody of their own, so did the Provençal weavers invent their own textiles based upon fabrics imported from the Orient. Eventually they created fabrics and patterns that are now identified with Provence and only with Provence. This began when cloths from India were imitated by weavers in Avignon and Tarascon despite a curious papal interdict against the practice. The industry flourished then and flourishes now under the manufacturing labels of Olivades and Soleiado. Stores, boutiques, and open markets are stocked with distinctively dyed (one color at a time) and patterned (invariably geometric) bolts that can be transformed into tablecloths, place mats, skirts, blouses, shirts, umbrellas, draperies, cushion and sofa covers, crimped caps on miniature cruets of breakfast jams and jellies, and sock-sized packets that contain herbs of Provence or lavender.

An equally indigenous and related craft that is centered in Cogolin near St. Tropez is the weaving of tapestries, carpets, place mats and other domestic textiles. Paul Clavier, the financial director of Tapis de Cogolin, explains during my tour of the factory that his staff of thirty women is in a slack period at the moment, working only four days instead of the usual five. He blames this on the economic climate, not only in France but also internationally, but adds that the women are paid for five days regardless. Behind him are bins of carded and dyed spools of white, pink, blue, yellow, and red wool. All of the wool is from France, chemically dyed and then woven by hand in either the old or the modern process. In the old method each woman weaves at a loom, compressing one horizontal thread at a time. In this way she can weave approximately two meters a day of finished fabric (all with geometric and not figurative designs). If she is exceptional, she might even be able to weave three meters. The modern method is to have artists trace a pattern on stretched and mounted backing after which a woman shoots threads from a wool-loaded gun into the already sketched patterns. Local artists have been contracted for this purpose, but Clavier possesses additional designs by Léger, Mondrian, and other famous artists. When you thank Monsieur Clavier for the tour, he tells you that many of his products are distributed in the United States by Brunschwig and that some are represented in the White House.

While still in Cogolin, I discover a small factory where smokers' pipes are carved. The owner is Charles Courrieu, whose son, Thierry, tells me that the Courrieu family has been in the business of handcrafting pipes since 1802. He proudly shows me framed photographs of the "old factory" in the same location taken almost a century ago. *Factory* is actually a misnomer. *Workshops* would more accurately describe the two kitchen-sized rooms where the pipes are spun on lathes, bored, balanced, stemmed with ebony or Lucite, and finally trademarked: "Courrieu Cogolin." All of the briar comes from the root burls of a heather-like bush that grows in the higher altitudes of the Maures so that the raw material is as local as the craftsmen— and one craftswoman. Thierry estimates that his eight employees, the best of whom seems to be the lone woman who bevels and burnishes the pipe bowls and shanks like jewelry on a buffing wheel, turn out 25,000 pipes a year. The prices vary from modest to hundreds of dollars for the artistic, fine-grained models. Thierry adds that there is a large "restoration or reparation" business where broken, impacted, or "sick" pipes are set right again. A well-stocked shop adjoins the factory. The whole enterprise shows no signs of depression despite the international movement *contre tabac*. Indeed the pipes of Cogolin are a genuine source of pride for the community as well as for France itself, and the palpable bond between *père et fils* indicates that there will be no petty squabbles at the top.

Another craft identified with Provence is the sculpting of glass, and it is practiced to a masterful perfection by the glassblowers of Biot, which is also famous for harvesting more than fifty tons of table grapes per year. From the central workshops of Biot have spun off highly individualized ateliers created by men who learned their crafts as apprentices and then struck out on their own. One of the best of these is Robert Pierini. On a stifling summer afternoon I visit him at his kiln with its adjoining boutique. Pierini is shaping a vase from a head-sized gob of hot glass fixed like a molten Q-tip to the end of a steel pole as long and thick as a broom handle. I watch him turn and tease the vase-to-be out of the gob, firing it again and again in the kiln, cupping it with one hand gloved in asbestos like a lover or sculptor palming a breast, spraying it, scissoring off the excess, beveling and leveling the base, smiling or frowning as the work goes well or stubbornly. He is forty-two, bearded *como un diablo* and built like a soccer goalie. He smiles the inward smile of a man to whom the achievement of perfection is the only human enterprise worthy of man's time and energy. Taking a break from the kiln, he gives you his fax number "in case." The businessman in him slowly surfaces but without insistence. He compliments me on my pathetic French as we converse, and I leave feeling as I always feel after I have talked with someone whose work and life are synonymous. I feel that some things are complete in this world.

The abundance of fine craftsmanship in textiles, briar, and glass (as well as olive wood) is more than balanced by Provence's wealth in the fine arts. It is not by accident that there are more art museums in Provence than in any comparable area in the entire world. Nor would it be inaccurate to say that many of the greatest artists of this century and before did some of their best work while they lived here. Their legacies have become tangible parts of the areas where they worked. Go to Arles, for example, and the name of Vincent Van Gogh is omnipresent as are reproductions of his paintings on posters, art paper, diaries, appointment calendars, and T-shirts. This latter form of exploitation is understandable as avarice's indebtedness to memory, but it is ironic that this Dutchman, who sold but one painting in his short and tragic life, is not represented by a single original painting in Arles or Provence. The irony intensifies when I visit the cloister and clinic of St. Paul in St. Rémy just below the stunning Roman ruins at Glanum. It was here that Van Gogh lived and painted after admitting himself for care by the resident doctors. Seeing Van Gogh's room is now forbidden. Even the bronze bust of Van Gogh by Zadkine was stolen by vandals in 1989. The pedestal that displayed the bust near the aisled entrance to the cloister remains. Beside it is a photograph of the bust together with a note in explicit French excoriating the thieves who stole it. It is as if Van Gogh's spirit is present only in hearsay.

What Van Gogh meant and means to Arles and St. Rémy is replicated in the link between Paul Signac and St. Tropez, Pierre Bonnard and Le Cannet, Pierre-Auguste Renoir and Cagnes-sur-Mer (where he painted to the end with paintbrushes taped to fingers stiffened like sticks because of advanced arthritis), Paul Cézanne and Aix-en-Provence, Jean Cocteau and Menton, Henri Matisse and Nice as well as Vence, Marc Chagall and St. Paul de Vence, and Pablo Picasso and Vallauris, Antibes, Cannes, and Mougins. These names are not merely a litany of the greatest artists of our time. These are the authors of paintings that unveiled Provence internationally to all those who learned of it first through their art. This proves again that most people do not truly see what they're seeing until it is seen for them in prospect or retrospect by the artist-seer. You cannot peruse the countryside around Aix-en-Provence or the whale-head contour of Mont Ste.-Victoire without seeing them as Cézanne saw them. The same holds true for Chagall and St. Paul de Vence. Look down from any window on the little cemetery at its base, where Chagall is appropriately buried, and you find yourself looking with Chagall's eyes at the above-ground stone gravemarkers festooned with ribboned bouquets, vased lilacs, or neatly cellophaned roses, jonquils, or carnations.

Not far from where D. H. Lawrence died in Vence, I visit the Blue Chapel of the Rosary, which Matisse created to thank the Dominican nuns who cared for him in their infirmary there. Standing before the raised, angled altar, I understand how spirituality can infuse art. It's in the simplicity of lines on the walls and a corresponding simplicity in the recently exhibited vestments that Matisse created for celebrants to don there. I see in these the same sure hand that created the "Nude with Orange" in the Pompidou in Paris; the subject changed but not the talent. The final tribute I feel obliged to pay after visiting the chapel is that Matisse, a nonbeliever who was at home with hippy odalisques in wanton sprawls, could and did create a space that actually induces prayer.

And then there is the Provence of Picasso, a Provence Mediterraneanized by this Catalán genius to whom France was an adopted country. But what Provence gave to Picasso, it received in return a hundredfold, not only in the work he bequeathed to it but also in what his art and generosity did for it. Like Mistral before him, Picasso contributed some of his largesse to support the Reattu Museum in Arles. And there was the way he reciprocated the kindness of the director of the Château Grimaldi, who let him use the château for half a year in 1945. In appreciation, Picasso bequeathed most of the work he did there to create what is now the Picasso Museum.

Picasso's flamboyance engendered numerous legendary stories, some apocryphal, some not. Rumor has it, for instance, that he moved out of his home in Cannes because a new apartment complex blocked his view of the sea. The daughter of his son Paulo now lives in it. Another anecdote is that Picasso and Françoise Gilot, his companion at the time and later the wife of Dr. Jonas Salk, had rented a villa for the summer from a French general. When the general returned, he found the walls splashed with paint. Picasso apologized, explaining that he and Françoise Gilot were "sloppy painters." To compensate, Picasso offered the general any painting of his choice free of charge. Despite the fact that Picasso's paintings at the time were selling for hundreds of thousands of dollars, the general is reported to have said, "No, thank you. I don't like your work."

The most serendipitous marriage between Picasso and Provence occurred when the ceramists Georges and Suzanne Ramié of the Madoura factory in Vallauris invited him to consider clay as an artistic medium. Picasso worked at the factory for one day (July 1, 1946), then returned one year later to the day to forge an alliance with the Ramiés that extended for twenty-five years in all. Some of Picasso's work in ceramics is on daily display in the Madoura factory and boutique. A complete historical catalogue of his total creation shows you dishes with human faces, platters on which toreros dare ceramic bulls, water pitchers whose handles are the ears of faces on the sides. The catalogue is the work of Alain Ramié, the son of Georges and Suzanne Ramié. Not a ceramist himself, Alain manages the various Madoura enterprises and is aware that he is involved not merely with a business legacy but "with history itself." He explains that Picasso himself prescribed the numbers for the limited editions he created in collaboration with Suzanne Ramié. Many are no longer available for sale. Those still for purchase have prices ranging from $500 to the astronomical. Asked if I might see the master ceramists at work (there are only three), Alain Ramié smiles and shakes his head, no. No observers are permitted, "jamais."

When I leave the Madoura factory and walk down Avenue Georges Clemenceau where the numerous pottery shops show no signs of depression, I pass the Avenue Pablo Picasso. Is this Vallauris's perfect tribute to a man who redeemed its major craft from gradual decline and did more for Vallauris than Georges Clemenceau ever dreamed of doing? Of course, I cannot forget that Picasso painted the Chapel of Peace here after numerous exhortations. The war panels of the painting seem repugnant to me, but why should I have assumed that war should generate beauty? And he also donated a sculpture called "Man with Goat" after it was inexplicably and stupidly rejected by the city officials of Antibes. Picasso insisted that the statue be situated in the midst of life. And it is. Visit the open market in Vallauris, and there it stands amid radishes, eggplants, cucumbers, tomatoes, cantaloupes, hucksters, and housewives. I assume that dogs can urinate on its base at night, exactly as Picasso said he wanted dogs to do.

But Picasso's most memorable contribution to Provence was to use a medium dug from the earth of Provence itself and transform it into objects where beauty and utility are one. You might even say that he perpetuated a craft that evokes the divine if one is willing to identify God as the original clay sculptor. In this spirit, Georges Ramié's tribute to Picasso, with all its baroque elegance, seems the most appropriate not merely because it is personal but also because it is timeless:

> With fitting reverence he approached this magical material, so sensitive to the mere stroke of the thumb yet so implacable in its reactions to the least variations of humidity, so stubborn in the hands of the uncomprehending yet so docile when treated with respect, a material so fragile while it is still in the shaping, totally dazzled from its recent metamorphosis to become from then on incombustible and imperishable, still to be purified by the terrible ordeal of fire. For here, indeed, this substance of so precious a humility becomes, by its permanence, the truest bearer of the message of mankind; however far back in time one goes, the evidence of humanity from the earliest epochs reaches us, not engraved in stone which crumbles to dust and erodes, not cast in metal which rusts and powders, but on little tablets of clay, with graphic signs as expressive today as when beneath the stylus of the scribe who traced them.

In due course, art museums followed the artists into Provence, and today they constitute a feast of feasts for amateur and professional alike: the Léger in Biot, the Fragonard in Grasse, the Chagall, the Dufy, and the recently refurbished Matisse in Nice, the already mentioned Picasso Museum in Antibes, the Renoir in Cagnes-sur-Mer, the atelier of Cézanne in Aix-en-Provence, to name only the most prominent among multiples of other less individualized collections.

The two museums that intrigue me the most are the Fondation Maeght in St. Paul de Vence and the Museum of the Annonciade in St. Tropez. The Fondation Maeght is really a stroll in the open air in the company of work by Pol Bury (a fountain of shifting silver tubes that tip and empty endlessly as a continual flow of water dictates), Calder, Chagall, Miró, Arp, and Giacometti, whose gaunt striders resemble naked penitents marching eternally toward God. All of these co-populate a park of trees, lawns, and incomparable cool shade. The entire space was designed by the Catalán architect José Luis Sert, but the real instigator was André Malraux, who persuaded Aimé Maeght to create and subsidize it. There is a rock-walled building complete with topping domes that houses the paintings, including a huge, dancing canvas by Chagall, a boutique, and a theater. But the unique beauty of the place is its leaf-canopied openness where one can amble or pause beneath umbrellas of pine and murmur an inward hello to sculptures and carvings that suddenly seem like one's closest friends.

The Museum of the Annonciade in St. Tropez exists in the very midst of bustle—a shrine of classical elegance beside the docked and softly bobbing yachts on one side and the *brasseries,* hair salons, card shops, pharmacies, and the tourist-jammed streets on the other. The present curator is Jean-Paul Monery, who did graduate work in Chicago on minimalist art and was a curator in Grenoble before coming to St. Tropez. Dissatisfied with St. Tropez itself, he has nonetheless written an opulent catalogue of the museum, which has a lot to be opulent about, plus a Gallimard guidebook for the entire area. Two names dominate his monologue as he describes the museum and its holdings—Georges Grammont, an industrialist and philanthropist who assumed the responsibility and expense of remodeling the chapel (originally Chapelle de Notre Dâme de l'Annonciade, built in 1510) into a museum in 1936; and Paul Signac, who came to St. Tropez by yacht in 1892, settled there for twenty years, and invited many of his fellow artists to work there for varying periods. Signac's talent and influence plus Grammont's philanthropy almost fifty years later have given the world one of the finest collections of Fauvist and other avant-garde paintings in one of the most tastefully restored spaces in France.

Monery explains certain voids: "Only half the collection is in the museum at one time. The absent half is on loan or on tour." I pass two life-sized bronze female nudes by Aristide Maillol, and I observe how Maillol's nudes are invariably without shame, exaggeration, or vanity. Then, Monery pauses before Pierre Bonnard's "Nude in Front of a Fireplace," one of the many paintings in which Bonnard's wife served as his model. I ask Monery to explain as an art historian why Madame Bonnard, on the evidence of the paintings alone, seemed to enjoy the condition of total nudity at home. Monery looks surprised. "But don't you know she had a condition . . ." He rubs the back of his hand. "How do you say in English? Dermatological? She had a skin condition. She could not tolerate even a *tissu* [fabric] on her skin. So she preferred to be naked in her own house." The result is that Bonnard simply painted her as he saw her.

Of course, there are smaller museums and ateliers all over Provence. One that deserves special mention is in Vence, the VAAS gallery and workshop in the restored art studio of Jean Dubuffet adjacent to what used to be his home. This is the fulfillment of a dream of Marion Duteurtre, who sold her gallery in Milan to create this space for the exhibition of new art, including the dramatic sculptures of Max Squillace and other Italian and French artists.

But the creation of beauty is not only the prerogative of artisans, writers, and artists in Provence. There are also the chefs. And the perfumers.

The cuisine of Provence, differentiated early on from other French cuisine by the Provençal option of using olive oil and garlic, is derived from a bountiful agriculture and *fruits de mer,* or seafood. Walk through any of the open markets, and you pass a cornucopia of all the raw materials that make good chefs salivate when they personally choose the day's foodstuffs: sagittal slices of dourade, pop-eyed loup beside flat-eyed sole, cheese by the loaf or wheel or wedge, barrels of mussels, overflowing bins of fresh green peppers, bunched parsley, potatoes in mesh sacks, cherries and table grapes asprawl, pyramids of the three Ps of Provence (*pommes, pêches, poires*—apples, peaches, pears), baguettes, croissants, corked glass quarts and gallons of pellucid olive oils with a sprig of herb immersed in each bottle, bushels of light green melons that have the taste of cantaloupe raised to the umpteenth power. Such open markets abound in every village, town and city. In the hands of chefs such as Jacques Chibois of the Gray d'Albion in Cannes, Jean-André Charial of the Beaumanière in Les Baux, Dominique Ferrière of the Château St. Martin above Vence, Jean-Yves Johany of Le Cagnard in Haut-de-Cagnes, Jacques Maximin of the Hôtel Negresco in Nice, Alain Ducasse of the Hôtel de Paris in Monaco, and the deservedly famous and widely revered Roger Vergé of Le Moulin de Mougins in Mougins, the fruits, vegetables, fish, and meats of Provence are transformed into masterpieces for the eye as well as for the palate.

French chefs are not only kings in their kitchens. They also have the standing of culinary artists in a country where gastronomy is taken seriously. Jacques Maximin, for example, received one of the highest awards that the national government can bestow, and the rarely given three-star Michelin rating is worn like a badge of honor by Micho and Lulu Barel at Le Cagnard in Haut-de-Cagnes as well as by Alain Ducasse and Roger Vergé. In France such citations are roughly equivalent to secular canonizations. Perhaps it derives from the Gallic belief that dining is the only human activity that activates all of the five senses simultaneously. Diners see the food, smell it, taste it, touch it, and enjoy the conversation of their fellow diners, all at the same time. Therefore, the great French chefs do not believe that dining should be taken lightly, despite the intrusions of McDonald's and Quick's into civic life. Beside the name of Escoffier, the master French chef from Provence whose name on sauces and cookbooks is known throughout the world and who has a museum commemorating his career in his birthplace at Villeneuve-Loubet, the fast fooders seem temporary. To the French and to gourmet cognoscenti everywhere the names of Escoffier and his successors are as well known as Nostradamus, Emile Zola, Alphonse Daudet, the Marquis de Sade, Garibaldi, all of them fellow Provençaux.

One afternoon I discuss restaurateurism at Les Muscadins in Mougins with Edward Bianchini, the Philadelphia-born director and manager of the hotel and restaurant. I begin by telling him that I noticed the restaurant was filled to capacity on the previous night when I ate there. "That took four years to develop," he says. He speaks slowly, as if reliving each of the four years. "Originally we opted for highly priced dinners, but I fought for reasonably priced complete meals, well presented and well served. For me this is the key to restaurant dining in Provence in the future. And, of course, it is essential to have a good chef."

Later I meet the chef, Noel Mantel. He has just prepared a special lunch of risotto with truffles, filets of mullet sprinkled with crushed olives on a bed of franc-thick zucchini slices, and a saddle of lamb ebbed with beans, onions, and shallots. He tells me that he has studied cooking from the age of fourteen and that he served his apprenticeship in the best hotels in Nice and St. Tropez. Every day he buys all the vegetables, fruits, fish, and meat for Les Muscadins and prepares the menus. He likes working in a small hotel where his authority and responsibilities are not restricted, except by the discipline of the work itself. I remember how Bianchini stressed the crucial importance of a good chef to restauranteurism. The shy, quiet-spoken, and precise young man opposite me looks vocationally at peace. And confident. And competent. He is twenty-four years old.

Among the numerous outstanding chefs in the south of France there is general agreement that the master chef is Roger Vergé. Together with Paul Bocuse in Lyons, Vergé has given French cooking an international stature that has enhanced tourism in the area. Many restaurateurs credit Vergé with focusing attention on Provence as a center for good food, and many of the leading chefs apprenticed with him early in their careers.

Preparing to meet Roger Vergé in Le Moulin de Mougins, I wish my knowledge of his books was more extensive. I know that his *Cuisine of the Sun* sold more than 100,000 copies in its English edition alone. I know that Vergé has subsidiaries in Disney World's Epcot and in Japan. I will learn that he has an ongoing cooking school in Mougins as well as a second restaurant, L'Amandier, a boutique for his oils and other condiments and a special outlet for his trademarked wines.

In person, Roger Vergé impresses me as a man who wears his honors lightly. With his white hair and white mustache, he could pass as someone's French uncle from the interior. But he converses with the ease of a man accustomed to interviews and not in the least hesitant to share what he knows. Because of numerous trips to the United States, his attractively accented English is idiomatic.

"To remain fresh we change our menu five times a year. For the businessmen's luncheon we change every week. Right now the economy is not as good as before. The *monnaie* is still there, but the people do not spend as much. This is why I have a less expensive menu at L'Amandier." He pauses to take a telephone call, which he handles with the ease and confidence of a man who makes pivotal decisions in his business habitually. "Today too many people ask the children not to be in the kitchen Why? I think children should be in the kitchen if they prefer. I am a chef today because my Aunt Célestine gave me a stool to stand on so I could watch her and help her." Another telephone call, which he terminates with polite dispatch. "For me, cooking is like the lines of a drawing. But the sauce is the color. You divide good chefs from ordinary chefs by the sauce. A good chef must be a good *saucier.*"

Later he leads me on a brief tour of the reconstructed mill known as Le Moulin de Mougins. "It has taken me twenty-five years to make what you see." There are original paintings and sculptures (one a compressed cube of old copper cooking pots) by Miró and César. There is a photograph of Salvador Dalí. There, one of Picasso. "Picasso rarely came, but I let him park his car in the lot." On the glass walls of an aperitif room are signatures of celebrities of note: Yves Montand, James Coburn, Anthony Quinn, Audrey Hepburn, and Elizabeth Taylor, to name a few. During the Cannes Film Festival in 1993, Elizabeth Taylor hosted an AIDS benefit dinner at Le Moulin for four hundred guests (including Michael Douglas, Sylvester Stallone, Jack Lang, Louis Malle, Kenneth Branagh, and an unbraceleted Adnan Khashoggi) in cooperation with Vergé. "Of all these actors and famous people, my favorite was Danny Kaye. He always came right into the kitchen. In the last of his life he gave everything to UNICEF. He was very generous. He always wanted to share. And I believe, like him, why are we here except to share?"

He talks briefly about a Peruvian girl he has adopted, about his recent friendship with Sharon Stone ("a good actress, but sometimes she has bad parts"), about the need for the constant diversification of menus. When I leave, he invites me to return for a meal as his guest. I tell him I'll take a raincheck. He frowns. The term is new to him. After I clarify the meaning, he smiles, shakes my hand, and says, "If we have rain or if we have no rain, come back. I will remember you."

I am surprised to learn, after many inquiries and investigations, that France's leading and most profitable export is perfume. Flowers are next, with high-tech computer products, textiles, and automobiles lower on the list.

The perfume industry actually owes its existence to a woman. To be more specific it owes its existence (as well as its continued existence) to the human nose. The original nose belonged to Catherine de Medici. After a visit to the area around Grasse, she suggested to the glovemakers there that the glove leather should be perfumed to counter its rank smell. They obliged. Instead of remaining glovemakers, they came to identify themselves as glovemaker-perfumers, then perfumer-glovemakers, and finally just perfumers. The face of Helen of Troy may have "launched a thousand ships," but in this case a woman's nose, albeit the nose of the destined wife of the king of France, launched an industry.

Centered in Grasse, which is the world capital of perfume, the perfumeries of Fragonard, Gallimard, Molinard, and others have made French perfumes synonymous with chic throughout the world. Perfumes have been created in other cultures, namely, the Egyptian, Greek, Roman, and Levantine, but Grasse established its preeminence by mixing alcohol with basic oils and floral essences to give the scents greater stability and longevity. Recently some chemicals have supplemented a few of the organic ingredients (Java patchouli oil, Indian ginger, vanilla, aniseed, ambergris, deer musk, civet from Ethiopian cats, and sandalwood, to list the most prominent). To make perfumes of the highest quality from this alphabet of ingredients is not a matter of potluck. It is a genuine science as well as a multimillion-dollar-a-year business.

It all begins with a "nose," the term used in the trade to identify someone whose sense of smell is acute and who has the talent to create new scents by intermarrying existing ones in different combinations. Of approximately three hundred "noses" throughout the world, fifty are in Grasse. To become an official "nose" one must attend a school for "noses" in Versailles. Two years of chemistry are required for graduation, further stressing the scientific core of the profession.

The president and director general of the Fragonard perfumery is Dr. Patrick Fuchs. Although he inherited the factory from his father, he has the requisite credentials for his position. He studied with Nobel awardee Dr. Robert Burns Woodward at Harvard and has a doctorate in chemistry. He tells me in his air-conditioned office, while hundreds of tourists and schoolchildren are touring the factory just beyond his door, that his father insisted on his attending Harvard so that Fragonard could be kept abreast of scientific developments related to the making of perfume. His father spoke from experience, having created a best-selling perfume for Elizabeth Arden called "Blue Grass."

"My brother Gilles did not want to be a perfumer," says Dr. Fuchs. "He has a doctorate in law from Oxford. But then he married the granddaughter of Nina Ricci. So now he is the president of Nina Ricci. One of life's ironies."

I learn from Dr. Fuchs and his staff that the making of perfume in many ways parallels the making of wine. Wine, by the way, is also an industrial staple in Provence with individual wines being identified with individual towns or regions. Provençal wines, even in the Var, are not in the class of the wines of Burgundy and Bordeaux, but they are not dismissable—the rosé of Tavel, for example. As tons of grapes are needed to create good wines, so is an abundance of flowers required to create the essences from which perfumes are made. Archibald Lyall calculates that the "coast produces some twenty thousand tons of mimosa, carnations, roses, jasmine, mignonette, narcissi, jonquils, tuberoses, and violets a year." In Antibes alone more than 9 million square feet are devoted to the growing of flowers. This is roughly the equivalent of one hundred city blocks.

Distillation soon makes short work of all this tonnage. Over two thousand pounds of jasmine, for example, are required to create thirty-four ounces of the *neroli* or essence of jasmine. Similarly, the required number of roses needed to make two and a quarter pounds of rose essence is ten million, approximately one ton. Two thousand

pounds of jasmine! Ten million roses! I try imagining such quanti-
ties in terms of feathers or ping-pong balls and then give up. And it
all boils down to two pounds of essence. Moreover, the jasmine and
roses must be picked between 4 AM and 11 AM so that the fragrance
will not be lost to the sun at its meridian and thereafter. Similar
care is required in the watering of the plants prior to picking. The
watering must be done at night by mask-wearing men who cannot
have eaten garlic or onions for fear that the odor will be inhaled by
the flowers. No wonder that a pound of essence has a price roughly
equivalent to its corresponding weight in gold. What an industry
hath Catherine de Medici wrought! Beautiful and sweet-smelling in
the blooming, providing employment in the harvesting and processing, and garnering profits in the marketing! The entire cycle strikes
me as self-sustaining, self-perpetuating, and derived from the environment itself. And all for the benefit of Grasse, Provence, and France.

I am standing on one of the parapets of Eze, a perched, or hilltop, village that gives you a view of the eastern reaches of Provence
as far as Menton in one direction and Antibes in the other. I wonder
what it is about this part of the world that has drawn people to want
to paganize themselves here. Is it because, as I've already noted,
Christianity here is less Pauline so that it permits an easier commerce
between the flesh and the spirit, a more sensuous and even more
sacramental view of life, and an acceptance of it on those terms, un-
sublimated and welcomed? Is it because the French insistence upon
individual taste as the bedrock of social life has its ultimate flower-
ing here? Or is it simply because this is a culture without a false bottom, physically speaking? For those who believe that a man is just
a mind, life starts from the top of the head and ends with the chin.
For Puritans, life ends at the waist. In Provence, it includes everything from the top of the head to the soles of the feet—a total view
that has created a way of life that it reflects honestly.

This is not to romanticize the place. All anyone has to do is read
Marcel Pagnol's *Jean de Florette* and *Manon of the Springs* or have seen
the excellent films based on them to get a hint of the mendacity
and avarice and venery that lie just below the surface. But such nega-
tives exist wherever man exists. Told by many to be watchful of my
valuables during my stay in Provence, I once hurried back to my car

where I had parked it fully loaded after having left the key in the door. Approaching the car and expecting the worst, I saw a young man approaching me with the key in his hand. "Monsieur," he asked, "are you searching your key?" He smiled modestly when I thanked him, shrugged off an offer of lunch as a small reward, and left. Nothing in the car had been disturbed.

Still, I can't overlook the disagreeable: the glitz of the Noga Hilton in Cannes, the acknowledged networking of the French Mafia from Marseilles into the interior, the seediness of the politics of Nice that Graham Greene publicly exposed and excoriated in *J'Accuse* in 1982 shortly before he died in Antibes, the pollution of the Mediterranean that a consortium (France, Italy, and Monaco) is desperately trying to reverse, the undisguised up-pricing in season of everything from sun-block nipple cream to a dish of strawberries.

But the real Provence is for those who trust in and hunger for the truths of the body and who discover these truths by surrendering to them. Provence does not reveal itself to the disembodied mind. It responds to those who see the world through the senses. It's what one feels when one views the Gorge of Verdon, France's Grand Canyon without the vastness. It's one's response to the long trek to Rocquebrune where Winston Churchill vacationed and William Butler Yeats died. I search Rocquebrune's hilltop cemetery until I find amid the baroque and bourgeois graves the blue, flat, natural-stone marker on which is scratched in French: "Here lies Edouard Jeanneret, known to the world as Le Corbusier." It's what is able to accommodate John Wayne's former villa in Antibes with its cowboy-hat roof and the restored Château St. Martin with its precise and priceless elegance. It's standing before the grave of Albert Camus in Lourmarin with its blackened stone marker on which his name is centered in capital letters along with the dates of his stay on this earth: 1913–1960. Other visitors follow me there as I am following those who preceded me. I think of more than forty years of visitors—the living's ultimate tribute to greatness.

It's sitting at a sidewalk table on the Cours Mirabeau in Aix-en-Provence. I am eating melon and sipping *café au lait* and appreciating the legacy of Good King René who planted the seeds for this university city in the fifteenth century. It's passing a small alley in Golfe-Juan that is marked inconspicuously as the beginning of the Route Napoléon. It's visiting the castle of Saint-Privat at the Pont du Gard where Richelieu stayed for a week to make allies of the owners whom his kind could not defeat. The current owner, Mrs. Jean-René Fenwick, is presently engaged in a legal skirmish with the government to keep its encroachments at bay. No counterpart of Richelieu has thus far been dispatched to pacify Mrs. Fenwick. The castle has a flavor of resisted decay while its gardens resemble the set of an Antonioni film. Still, it is more authentic than the castle at Ansouis, where mounted military portraits, swords, and general overdoneness makes you wish for a new Rousseau to turn such puffery upside down. As I am leaving the estate, I notice a number of bathers who are swimming downriver from the Pont du Gard or lounging on the irregular shores. In one secluded section a man and a woman, totally naked, are caressing, writhing, and kissing one another in complete indifference to the world at large. I wonder how long Mrs. Fenwick can defend herself and her estate against these more proximate encroachments. Or even if it matters.

It's standing in the beige-rock chapel of the abbey at Le Thoronet and letting the clash of silence and sunlight give you a different sense of your very self—a more resonant one, as if you've suddenly been underlined for emphasis. It's walking the interminable beaches of Ramatuelle and Pampalone where nakedness and near-nakedness evoke nothing but indifference. Bathers do not seem mistakenly unclothed but simply and frankly nude. It's walking in Eze. The village cats are sunning themselves on warm rocks. You pass two plaques in the cemetery with French male names on them; under each is the succinct phrase, *Victime des Nazis*. In other places in Provence you will see a street named after someone whose name means nothing to you. The name is followed by the word: *Resistant*, the modest French way of memorializing the members of the Resistance. A small detail, but significant. It's passing St. Raphaël and realizing that the invasion of the Riviera happened in this very vicinity in 1944 and not at Nice, where the Nazis were expecting it. It's coming to understand that Provence is indeed a "feeling" as much as it is a place that invites and rewards revisiting. "I could never let a year go by without traveling there for a few weeks at least. Provence is a taste or more correctly a passion which once contracted cannot be cured," wrote James Pope-Hennessy, one of Provence's best biographers. And Bo Niles, the author of *A Window on Provence*, responded in a similar spirit when she wrote about her stay there near Ménerbes: "I love the fragrances: lavender, of course, and rosemary. The colors—even if they are bleached by noon; at sunrise and sunset they are exquisite and intense. I love the trees: olive, cypress, plane trees, cherry, and the vegetables, abundant in the markets and garden. The sound of cicadas. The long days."

Mysteries always elude definition in the same way that great paintings seem unframeable even when they are framed. Such is Provence, elusive but true, and real as the wind. Or rather the six winds: the *levante* from the east; the *gregaou* with its hail; the northerly *tramontana;* the two sisters from the south, the *sirocco* and the *libeccio;* and, finally, the mistral, which originates in the Alps and rushes down the Rhône valley like an invisible avalanche.

The first time I encountered the mistral was when I was in Avignon. My wife and I were strolling toward our hotel when the evening breeze suddenly seemed to stiffen and then change key, as if in response to a direct order. Within minutes we had to lean our bodies forward just to keep our balance. The knifing, slashing gusts careened through the labyrinthine streets of that walled city as if the very air were in flood. Blown-down leaves swirled against store windows and into gutters, where they huddled like terrified sparrows. Then the mistral climaxed, axing down branches and cartwheeling signs through the deserted square. Those signs that the mistral could not unhinge slammed against their moorings again and again, like sailcloth snapping and shredding in a hurricane. The wind settled— a threatening calm—and then charged back as an enraged bull might charge after a respite. And all the while, the mistral whined and whistled like a chorus of flutes played by the insane.

The mistral, whose name comes from *magister,* the Latin word for *master,* is a distinctive part of Provençal life, punctuating the region's otherwise congenial climate. It appears throughout the year, unpredictably and without warning. The force of the mistral is generated when the dry, cold Alpine winds above the northern Rhône valley clash with the warm winds on the Alps' southern side. If there is a drop in barometric pressure, the warm winds yield, and the chilly gusts come barreling down the length of the Rhône valley, not stopping until they reach the African continent.

Short of being caught in one, the most immediate way to learn about the mistral is to talk with residents—permanent ones if possible, seasonal if not. The permanent residents invariably begin with the conventional wisdom. They say that it is a "mud eater" whose arid currents suck up puddles from fields and dirt roads. And they claim that it blows itself out in multiples of three if it begins during the day (three days, six days, and so on) but lasts only long enough to be an annoyance if it rises by night.

What the mistral is most noted for is its ability to put people on edge. It makes people nervous. It causes the eyes to smart and tear. Stendhal called it the "greatest drawback" to a stay in the south of France. And it's bloody loud. This probably explains why the shutters on Provençal windows seem thicker than shutters elsewhere; nothing decorative here. However hospitable the appearance of unshuttered windows may be to the outside world, the shutters can close up a house like a box when the mistral passes through, sealing out both sight and, one hopes, sound.

There is an island in the Mediterranean (possibly Sardinia) where the inhabitants refer to their version of the mistral as "the whip." The figure is apt, since a genuinely strong wind lashes nature, man included, into submission. Since no one likes to be enslaved, a wind can make rebels out of those it subdues. It is resented. It creates defenses and accommodations. There are, for example, almost no stone belfries in the south of France, the theory being that the mistral will eventually dislodge the stones. The Provençal alternative is the bell cage, in which the bell is hung and swung and rung. The iron bars of the cage permit the wind to blow through and dislodge nothing at all.

The personal counterpart of such accommodation is resignation. One hotel proprietress near Vence looked puzzled when I asked her for her most vivid memory of a mistral, any mistral. "There was a tree that was blown down last year, and I think we lost a few shingles." She gave a French shrug, the kind that suggested how minor a place the mistral had in her scheme of things.

After the mistral has had its three-day, six-day, or nine-day fling, it leaves everything with a rinsed look. I noticed this the day after I experienced my Avignon mistral. While I was driving toward Uzès, I saw that the sky seemed to have been washed as clean as a windshield. The streets and roads shone. The formerly passive facades of buildings and houses actually seemed to be asserting themselves. The grass was definitely greener, but many trees along the road were permanently bent toward the south after decades of being pummeled by repeated mistrals.

To speak finally of the mistral is to borrow the spirit conveyed by the aforementioned French shrug. After all, Provence is a part of the world that is blessed with fertility, a predominantly temperate climate, and a special Mediterranean light. Its beauty, excellent cuisine, and civilized pace attract visitors from everywhere and keep faithful residents from leaving. Perhaps the mistral is the counterbalance. Its annoyances only intensify our immense appreciation of Provence's many natural gifts by reminding us that nature can intervene at times and places of its own choosing, even in gardens reminiscent of Eden. And when it does, we become like the classical Romans, who believed in the primary virtues of patience and perseverance in the face of what one cannot control. We shrug. We accommodate. We go on living.

The mistral and its five fellow winds seem to be symbolic of Provence. They blow where and when they will, shaping and forging a people as well as a climate and a geography. If they cannot be confined by lines on a map, then it is because they are as elusive as mysteries. And mysteries can never be imprisoned within a definition. They are knowable only when they are acknowledged and appreciated and loved. That is how it is with Provence. And that is how it should be.

Why Go Anywhere Whenever?

I am writing these lines while I am on vacation in order to explain (primarily to myself) why I dislike vacations. Not this particular vacation necessarily, but vacations in general or, if you will, the very idea of a vacation. Let me admit from the start that there may be something historical behind my antipathy. In my middle and late teens and into my mid-twenties I rarely thought of a vacation. I was too busy being a student or working or, for a two-and-a-half-year period, being first an enlisted man and subsequently an officer on active duty in the Marine Corps. The very idea of a vacation seemed to me a distraction from my primary interest or my primary occupation and responsibility, as the cases were then.

Shortly after I was married, I was persuaded by my wife, who loves to travel and to whom vacations are almost a necessary tonic, that it was time we took a vacation. At that time it happened to be a trip to the Adirondacks. And she has been persuading me ever since, as she did most recently for a midwinter week in Cancún on the Mexican coast. It is in Cancún that I am writing these words. Had she not suggested this trip, I am quite sure I would never have thought about it, with the result that I would not be here nor would I be writing what I am now writing.

My wife's reasons for our vacations have always been roughly the same. She will say, "It's time we take a vacation because we need it." Or she might say, "A change of scene will do us a world of good. It's necessary and important to go away and get some perspective, to see how the rest of the world lives." As a writer, I know that there is really no way to get away. Unlike a dentist or a doctor or a lawyer, I carry my profession in my very person. The result is that *there* becomes *here* when I get there, and what was once *here* becomes *there*. I remain myself despite the change in location. So why go anywhere whenever? Where am I when I'm *there* (wherever *there* is) but *here* and vice versa? Regardless of my quaint wordplay, I usually acquiesce to my wife's logic of self-interest and go. And in most cases her advice is proved correct by the trip. I return somewhat renewed, slightly tanned, and, in most instances, glad I went.

But being glad I went and being anxious to get away in the first place are not synonymous. I am almost never anxious to get away. My discomfort usually begins by allowing the notion of departure to monopolize my pre-departure thoughts. Gradually it usurps most if not all of my attention. It puts a kind of terminus on what I am doing at the moment, giving it a deadline that it was never intended to have by nature, making it seem not only temporary but also rather unimportant. The future then is no longer open-ended but infringed upon by a date of departure and a date of return. Also, the very imminence of leaving makes me more conscious than I care to be about my own mortality. I can't explain why. It's not the fear of flying in the Jungian and not the Jongian sense, although that fear does make itself felt in the anticipatory phase of anyone's trip. Nor is it the dread that "something might happen" at home while we are away or even that something untoward might happen to us in a strange city or country, although both of these forebodings are there as well. I can't explain the reason why I harbor these and related anticipations, but they are certainly there, and the preparation for travel accentuates them in the same way that it makes me feel older and more naked to fate than I would like to feel.

But there are finite annoyances that gnaw at me as well. Although I am a sincere admirer of handsome luggage, I loathe the act of packing and then hefting packed bags hither and yon. Let me add that

I am even less attracted by the act of unpacking. It's not that I'm not good at one or the other; I consider myself a rather good packer, usually erring on the side of underpacking rather than overpacking, but I dislike doing it even while I am doing it.

I dislike as well the haggling over ticket prices, assigned seats, hotel dates, hotel prices, restaurant prices, car-rental fees, taxes, currency rates of exchange, and gratuities. Language differences and difficulties actually bother me much less, even if they arise from languages I do not know, because I have found that the only vacations that truly constitute a change for me are those where I find myself in a totally different culture, and different languages are a key to that difference.

The unavoidable adjustment to time changes is a bother as well. Jumping your watch ahead when you are traveling from the United States to Europe or turning the clockhands back when returning or when continuing to travel farther west involves more than just a mind-change or kidney adjustment. It takes me weeks to return to my own clock after such sojourns in either direction, and I have difficulty in being philosophical about it, going or coming.

Hovering over all of these ineluctable annoyances is a basic question of identity. Or perhaps I should say the loss of identity. I know many people who quite literally enjoy "losing themselves" as long as the losses are temporary. They look forward, for example, to the feeling of anonymity they experience when they visit New York or London or Paris. I myself see nothing attractive about such hiatuses, and it is for this and several other aforementioned reasons that I almost resent being a tourist—not merely being regarded as a tourist by others but regarding myself as a tourist as well. To me it means floating through a society on a pay-as-you-go basis, concentrating on natural or manufactured sites, and doing certain things not for the sake of doing them but for the sake of having done them. This, to me, is like reading a book not for the joy of reading it but only for the sake of saying that you read it.

The devil's advocate in me forces me to even the scales at this point. Have I ever been in a country where certain things happened "along the way" that became permanently valuable and would never have been part of my life otherwise? The answer is yes. Through mere chance or serendipity I have met people who are now good friends of long standing. In one case this resulted in my becoming the godparent with my wife of one couple's children. In another instance I met with the late Swiss essayist and federalist Denis de Rougemont. Having been an ardent admirer of his classic *Love in the Western World*, I was able through this meeting to learn from him that one of his books of essays had not been translated into English. I volunteered to translate it, and he happily agreed. I say with all the fallibility at my command that the book would possibly not have been translated otherwise.

In the late 1970s I happened to be in Monaco and was fortuitously put in touch with Princess Grace. This unplanned meeting fructified into a friendship and made possible my inviting her to give the first of two poetry readings in the United States—readings that would not have happened without that initial fortunate contact. In Greece, again by the purest chance, I met the novelist Vassilis Vassilikos. I subsequently invited him to give a lecture at the International Poetry Forum in Pittsburgh on contemporary Greek poetry. He was en route to the United States to give the lectures when the junta toppled the Greek government. Vassilikos could not return to Greece for nine years. Had he been in the country when the junta assumed power, he almost assuredly would have been imprisoned, and his famous novel called *Z* would never have been published. Or once, while changing planes in Paris on my way to Nice, I met and had an airline-sponsored lunch with James Baldwin, learning in that brief period how incisive, provocative, and yet how spoiled (as an indulged, fawned-over, and indulgent boy is spoiled) he was. And there are numerous friendships I can ascribe to the same combination of luck and location that only travel can create. And there are poems I have written (as well as two novels) that I would never otherwise have written had I not been at a certain time in Mexico, Switzerland, France, Greece, Lebanon, Egypt, or Jamaica.

I suspect that my discomfort at being a tourist may be traceable to the fact that it heightens a sense of alienation I experience simply by being a stranger in someone else's country. In any case, alienation is not a state of being that I easily accommodate to, this side of outright necessity, and I find that travel only exacerbates the difficulty.

Travel also leaves me restless. My father, a merchant who traveled constantly during his life—indeed, his life *was* travel—once told me that traveling made it virtually impossible for him to change his life habits; it made it equally impossible for him to stop and put down roots anywhere permanently. There was always the lure of the horizon. But as a person to whom home has always meant more than a mere house with assorted creature comforts, I feel that my "restlessness" on the road may be traceable to the fact that I find myself somewhere that is, for me, inferior to what I have left behind, no matter how attractive and well-appointed the new place may be. I have this feeling of restlessness even when my wife and son are with me, so that it is not merely a question of family solidarity that can subsume it. It is something that remains a mystery to me even though its reality is as certain to me as the air I am breathing at this moment.

My antipathy to travel is further intensified when I listen to people to whom travel is an ultimate desideratum. Some of these people are those who travel for travel's sake alone and whose travel tales seem to have no other purpose than to arouse the envy or at least the curiosity of the not-so-well-traveled listener. Have you been to Florence? They've been there countless times, of course. Have you set foot on the Galapagos? They have, and they have the photographs to prove it. Have you bought gloves in Rome, linen in Madeira, scrimshaw in the Azores? They have. The litany is as endless as it is sterile. In the final estimate these travelers are really nothing more than consumers—the relatively new international consumers of the world at large considered as a product, bringing back as gossip or photographs the cultural creations of others. In the end they travel, as Czeslaw Milosz noted, "to acquire the language of snobbism,"

Away from home I invariably feel that I am living either on borrowed or regretted time. This manifests itself in the habit I have of counting the days when I am away until I begin the return trip. Alastair Reid has captured this feeling succinctly in his "Notes on Being a Foreigner" from his book *Whereabouts*:

> Tourists are to foreigners what occasional tipplers are to alcoholics—they take strangeness and alienation in small exciting

doses and besides, they are well fortified against loneliness. More-over, the places they visit expect and welcome them, put them-selves out for their diversion. Boredom is the only hazard—it takes a healthy curiosity to keep tourists from rushing home in tears, from sighing with relief at the reappearance of familiarity. The principal difference between tourists and foreigners is that tourists have a home to go to, and a date of departure. I wonder how many of them would confess to having found the pinnacle of pleasure from a trip in the moment of returning home? How appropriate tourists are, in certain places, at certain seasons. The only thing that sets them apart is that they have to invent rea-sons for visiting the places they visit, or else suffer from pointless-ness. And the sun, they discover, is not quite sufficient reason for being anywhere.

In this passage Reid has captured the central difficulty I have with being a tourist: dealing with ennui. This invariably has the ef-fect of convicting either the trip or me of maximum uninterest or maximum boredom, and since I lack the largeness of soul to make the best of a bad time, I tend to ignore or denigrate much of what is happening around me, particularly if it's regarded as exciting. Ex-citement represents to me unanticipated or false stimulation. When I am with people who are looking for something exciting to do, I usually find reasons to be elsewhere. What all this means is that I am not a man who is looking for *something* or who travels in order to complete and fulfill himself. Other places are invariably just other places to me. They represent neither salvations nor paradises. What I have found is that I discover new places with no preconceptions whatsoever. Thus, everything impresses itself upon me with equal or almost equal emphasis. The consequence is that I tend to remem-ber with better clarity than most gung-ho travelers numerous details about the passing scene that they tend to overlook. This tendency echoes a dictum of Marianne Moore in her famous poem about po-etry, in which she notes that "there are things that are important beyond all this fiddle," but that coming to it with perfect contempt may permit it to yield to us something valuable despite our con-tempt. And in the same vein, wasn't it Pascal who said that "the best philosophers hate philosophy"? If this can be transposed to read that the best travelers hate travel, I would reluctantly rank myself high on that list.

Traveling "to get away" is a movement of rarely recent vintage. Most travel historians credit Thomas Cook (of Cook's Tours) with making such travel both respectable and affordable for the middle classes of this world. Since then, Cook has had legions of imitators on all continents, and the American two-week vacation, like the French August shutdown, almost presumes that one must vacate one's premises for all or part of that time. Travel in this sense almost qualifies as a liberal art. Being done for its own sake, it is quite literally its own reward. It differs markedly from travel done for reasons of commerce, exploration, battle, discovery, relocation, emigration, immigration, learning, nutrition, or voluntary exile. While some laud the current opportunities for world travel at jet speed (what is more consoling or reassuring than knowing that one can board a jet at noon in Madrid and, barring mishaps, delays, or cancellations, sleep in one's own bed in Pennsylvania by midnight?), I suspect that these blessings might benefit more from skepticism than enthusiasm.

If one learns the art of compensation from globetrotting, all well and good. If one comes to identify the weaknesses in one's own culture when compared to the strengths in other cultures, so much the better. If one comes home with a renewed awareness of the common humanity of all people, then that is the best result of all. Most travelers, however, simply regard the proximity of other parts of the world by air as a convenience, nothing more. The aforementioned routine flight from Madrid to the United States, after all, covers the same distance that required three months of arduous travel by Thomas Jefferson's ambassador to Spain just over two centuries ago. Do today's travelers learn from travel? I don't know. One writer-in-exile noted a few years ago that one is not fully human until one realizes that one is not simply a citizen of a particular country but a citizen of the world, but he did not say if travel was a prerequisite for such knowledge. In my more self-congratulatory moments I tell myself that being a citizen of my country (and by differing degrees of commitment a citizen of my state, my city, my township, etc.) is a full-time job and that "vacation travel" is often a luxury I can't afford, not because of money but because of time. In my less noble but hence more human moments, I wonder if the only thing that deters me is the inconvenience.

But the chief value of travel for me is the deeper appreciation it gives me of home. Speaking allegorically for a moment, I see this as one of the reasons that makes baseball my favorite sport. The whole purpose of the game is for a runner to travel hopefully from home to home (from home plate and back to home plate). All the singles, doubles, and triples, statistics notwithstanding, count for nothing unless a runner comes home. Understand this, and you are well on your way to understanding Homer's *Odyssey*. For Homer's Odysseus, Ithaca was the point of departure as well as the point of return. The lands of Calypso, Circe, and the lotus eaters were not destinations but delays. They were, if you will, the first, second, and third bases of classical mythology, pauses en route. For me, my home (as well as the very idea of home) has that kind of magnetic Ithaca-pull. No matter where I stop, I never am fully myself until I return to live within my own walls; it is where, in the words of Philip Booth, we can "climb back Eden's hill" in our own backyard. If life is an exile, then home is where our alienation is least noticeable and consequently most bearable.

How can I conclude except to say that when I hear of a travel agency called Please Go Away (and there is such an agency), I am more impressed by the cleverness of the title than by what the title is asking me to do. Perhaps this homing instinct is traceable to the fact that I tend to live in full—physically, spiritually, and intellectually—wherever I am. By this I mean that I don't have the psychology or temperament that enables some people to tiptoe through life. No matter where I am, I sense my full self and weight within me, like an infantryman. Since being a tourist requires one to be a kind of Fred Astaire and since I am more inclined to emulate the foot soldier, I feel vaguely out of sorts on tours since every tour wants to be taken not as seriously in depth as I want to take it. In fact, I persist in wanting to take it quite seriously from start to finish, since every tour is in a real country with a real history and real problems, and this often leaves me looking like the one man on the dance floor who can't or won't polka. That same streak may have been responsible for my dating habits while I was single. Every girl I dated assumed the role of a potential mate. When it became apparent that for one reason or another she was not a potential mate, I saw no further reason to ask for a date. And I didn't. Again the demon of seriousness spared me the folly of Don Juanism or at least showed me that Don Juanism had nothing to promise in my future but more of the same—endless sampling but no choice, looking but never really stopping to see. As a tourist I seem to exemplify the same trait. I can never take travel heavily enough to get good at it, and I can't take it lightly enough to get the most out of it while it's happening, except in the negative sense of remembering a great deal about where I've been. No Ibn Battuta, I leave the world I've yet to see to its current inhabitants. If I see them, I see them. If not, so be it. But, in the spirit of the nomad I am not, I can say with a nomad's sense of hospitality that as visitors they are welcome in my house any time.

Remembering Gregory Peck

Gregory Peck died at the age of eighty-seven on June 12, 2003, and with him died a unique quality of confident reserve that few other actors, and even fewer people generally, seem to possess. His craggy good looks and his resonant basso-baritone made him internationally recognizable. His film saga began when he took a train to California as Eldred Gregory Peck and became, dropping a *prénom* he disliked, Gregory Peck. It began on screen when he was cast as a guerrilla leader in his first film and uttered his first screen line when he faced a fellow guerrilla suspected of being drunk: "Breathe on me." From that time on, Gregory Peck benefited from instant recognition.

My wife and I experienced such a moment of recognition at close quarters on a visit to New York. We boarded a hotel elevator for the lobby when the elevator stopped en route to permit a man and woman to board. The man, who was wearing a herringbone coat with a hat to match, was quite tall, and the woman (we learned later that it was his daughter) was conversing with him quietly. After we reached the lobby and went our separate ways, my wife told me that she was certain that he was Gregory Peck. I disagreed, stating that the man had a cropped, black mustache and that Gregory Peck never had a cropped, black mustache. (As we also learned later, Peck was in makeup at that time as the satanic Nazi doctor in *The Boys from Brazil*, and he had driven to New York for the weekend from Bucks County in Pennsylvania where the final scenes of the movie were being shot.) My wife and I proceeded to the hotel garage to retrieve our car, and there ahead of us was the mustachioed man I did not believe was Gregory Peck. As soon as he spoke to the attendant, I recognized the voice and realized that my wife was right all along. By then she had already approached him and was conversing with him, reminding him of a visit he had made to Pittsburgh the previous year with his wife Veronique when Heinz Hall was dedicated. Peck thanked her and smiled, remembering.

More than two decades later I invited him to appear at the International Poetry Forum. Having scripted a program of the poetry of William Butler Yeats, interspersed with instrumental Irish music, songs, and narration, I thought that the program might interest him. After he read the script, he faxed his cryptic answer, "You do the narration. I'll be Yeats."

Peck's Irishness was not something he flaunted, but it was a deep and constant presence for him, and he never took it for granted. He enjoyed trips to Ireland, and he told me that on a recent trip he could not help but notice how many of the men in Galway and elsewhere seemed to resemble him with their grayish or whitening hair and their black eyebrows. His interest in education even prompted him to fund a scholarship in his name for drama students at Trinity College in Dublin. Perhaps this connection was forged when Peck as a boy lived for a time in Ireland. His Irish mother returned there briefly after separating from her husband.

Peck told me several anecdotes with Irish overtones, but two in particular stand out. The first had to do with the filming of *Moby-Dick*. (It was for me the only film of Peck's in which he seemed to be miscast, but I never told him that. John Huston, who directed the film, should have cast himself as Ahab and been done with it.) In the final and decisive scene of the whale chase, Peck had to be lashed to the back of the synthetic Moby-Dick. Cameras began to roll. Just then a dense fog developed, and the prop whale with Peck roped to it drifted off into the Irish Sea with the film crew in vain pursuit. Hours later, Peck was miraculously rescued by some Irish fishermen, who must have been more than slightly amazed to come upon an American actor adrift in character on a runaway whale. In telling the story, Peck laughed it off in the same spirit in which he laughed off his portrayal of General Douglas MacArthur's return to the Philippines in the filming of *MacArthur*. It was a matter of historical record that MacArthur insisted on wading ashore when he came back to the islands with other military and civilian officials. He was also prominently smoking his trademark corncob pipe while he did so. In the re-creation of the scene in the movie, Peck was standing at the prow of the LST with his fellow actors. He was preparing to wade ashore à la MacArthur when the ramp was lowered. Down came the ramp, and Peck and his coterie stepped off into eighteen feet of water. They were all washed ashore eventually, and Peck, soaked to the skin, marched up the beach with the corncob pipe clenched defiantly in his mouth.

The second story had to do with his friend and fellow actor, James Mason. According to Peck, Mason did not have many stories, but he favored one in particular. It so happened that Mason was making a film near Dublin, and one evening he took time off to saunter in the downtown area. While he walked and window-shopped, he caught the attention of a woman who was doing the same thing. Finally but hesitantly the woman approached Mason, smiled, and asked, "Excuse me, sir, but could you be Mr. James Mason in his later years?" Peck explained that Mason appreciated the inquiry because it was both accurate and polite in the high Irish style.

In any event, Peck did accept my invitation to read the poems of Yeats in Pittsburgh in a program called "Horseman, Pass By." The response was quite enthusiastic, although Peck told me afterward that he was not satisfied with his performance. He said that he had worried too much about poetic values and poetic correctness and had not really inhabited each poem in the way an actor is capable of inhabiting a role by subordinating his own personality to the character being enacted. A year later, when Peck appeared in Pittsburgh for a theatrical benefit, he recited from memory and with genuine feeling Yeats's signature poem "Easter, 1916." I felt that it was his way of redeeming what he considered inadequate in his first presentation.

The last thing he told me before he left Pittsburgh for Los Angeles after his original reading was to call him if I were ever invited to recite my poetry in California and, if he were in town, he would be happy to introduce me. Two years later I did receive an invitation from Pomona College in Claremont, and he indeed did appear and did introduce me, an act whose total generosity and unselfishness I will never forget.

Over the remaining years of his life we stayed in touch sporadically—I by letter and he by fax, his preferred medium. We exchanged gifts at Christmas (he and his wife Veronique sent French bread from a select bakery in New York, and we sent Lebanese pastries). Peck became so addicted to the pastries that he became a permanent customer of the confectioner in Sterling Heights, Michigan, who made them. Years later, in a posthumous profile of Peck that was the main feature of the magazine *Irish in America,* he is quoted telling his interviewer to relax and help himself to some Lebanese pastries.

Peck is rightly honored for his many films, particularly for his identifying role of Atticus Finch in Harper Lee's *To Kill a Mockingbird.* (He and Lee became lifelong friends as a result of the film.) But his role as the Air Force general in *Twelve O'Clock High* contains a remarkable scene in which Peck, after disciplining and inspiring his entire squadron to near perfection, has an unanticipated nervous breakdown while attempting to vault himself into his command bomber for his final flight. He literally cannot force his body to obey him, and the camera captures the shock and impotence in his face with absolute clarity. Martin Scorsese has called this scene one of the most gripping and compelling in the history of film.

One could write extensively of Peck's devotion to his wife Veronique and their two children, Anthony and Cecilia, and also to his sons from his first marriage, including the one son, the ex-Peace Corpsman who took his own life and to whom Peck referred as "the boy we lost." But the quality of character that truly identified Peck and defined him as a man of reason and commitment was his willingness to stand up in public for his private convictions—personal, dramatic, cultural, or political. And there was always an almost stately modesty about him. When he received the Lifetime Achievement Award from the Academy of Motion Picture Arts and Sciences, he was caught on camera as he listened appreciatively to the many tributes his fellow actors were paying him including a particularly touching one from Audrey Hepburn. She remembered that it was Peck who had insisted that the name of Audrey Hepburn, a complete newcomer, receive equal billing with him in *Roman Holiday*. She won an Academy Award for her performance and did not forget the man who had made it possible for her. After the accolades were completed, Peck came to the dais to acknowledge them. He thanked his directors for "teaching him a lot—not everything, but a lot." He thanked with equal generosity all those who had given their testimonials. Then he looked directly at his wife in the audience and said, with just the right blend of private affection intended for public disclosure, "Veronique, you're the only girl for me. I'll see you later."

Almost a year after his death I learned from Eva Marie Saint that Peck was buried, or rather interred, in the crypt of the new Cathedral of Our Lady of the Angels in downtown Los Angeles. I promised myself that I would pay my respects, however belatedly, if and when I came to California. Finally, in 2004 the opportunity presented itself.

People had warned me that the cathedral was something you either liked or disliked. There was no middle ground. At the cost of approximately $200 million, suffice it to say that the cathedral strongly resembles a medieval Spanish armory. Its exterior of tan precast rocky slabs and its cavernous but minimally lighted interior create a sense of anything but welcome. The effect is almost sepulchral, and what windows there are look as if they were intended for an upscale warehouse. But the crypt or mausoleum under the main floor creates the exact opposite feeling. The lighting is indirect but plentiful, and the central promenade that bisects the vertically designated burial chambers in separate aisles is immaculate. The bishops of Los Angeles are commemorated with individual entablatures, including the current bishop whose life dates at this writing contain only the month and year of his birth. In one of the other aisles are two burial plaques for a man and his wife, he identified as "loving," she as "beloved." Since the church is new, there are not that many crypted tenants. In one of the central aisles there is a single occupant at present: Gregory Peck, 1916–2003. There is an aura of lonely nobility about it, much like the man himself.

TEN

To Wrestle a Slow Thief

How do I love thee? Let me count the lightbulbs. Counterclockwise is how I unscrew the dead ones. Clockwise is how I screw in their replacements. I can't begin to count the times I've played my part in this ritual of death and renewal, which tells me with every twist of my wrist that burning out is the price of burning bright. This is brought home to me by the prosaic 60-watters in the ceiling fixtures, the golf-ball-sized 40-watt globes over the bathroom mirror, the tri-watted (50-100-150) reading bulbs that somehow never expire all at once, the all-weather spotlights at the house corners that illuminate the lawn at midnight like searchlights questioning the sea, the petite white Christmas-tree cones that bloom under nightlight cowlings, the bulbs in the oven and the refrigerator that awaken when you open the doors and then go back to sleep when you close them. And finally there are the fluorescent cylinders that snap into their brackets, blink, and then sizzle purple-white as if they will shine forever.

All this is part of every house-owner's love story. Everyone knows that you draw closer to something when you minister to its deficiencies. Owners of old cars wax far more romantic about them and their ailments than those mere "steerers" of brand new models.

Why? Because what is less than perfect needs constant attention, and attention to anything breeds its own concoction of love, disappointment, and, above all, attachment. Some might even call it intimacy. So it is with houses. Constantly on call to repair failings or respond to emergencies of one kind or another, house-owners feel an attachment to their homes. At least I do. I may have borrowed to buy the house I live in and now own, but from the beginning it owned me. Now we cleave. It's small wonder, then, that in Western law most crimes against property are second only to crimes against person. In time, houses do become an extension of our personalities. They are more than real estate. They become part of ourselves. And they continually present us with bills for their maintenance and care whether we are ready or not. Perhaps for this reason an old French proverb reminds us that "a house is a slow thief."

Most of the problems with houses spring from wear. Things wear down, wear through, wear thin, wear loose, wear wrong, wear out. Some of these weardowns are fairly predictable. The life of a roof (except for tile shingles) is approximately twenty-five years. Almost all other wear-outs are proportionate to use. These breakdowns usually happen without warning, and every breakdown evokes a different kind of pain or chagrin. Take the water tank, for example. The failure of a water tank is usually timed to happen when you are taking a shower or about to take one in preparation for one of the most important events in your life. You notice that the shower spray is gradually turning colder until it finally reaches an Arctic low. After examining the water tank and tapping its sides to the accompaniment of some rather choice basement blasphemy, you call a repairman and wait. By luck he happens to be in your "area" so you are spared a purgatorial delay.

You may turn out to be lucky—shortsighted, but lucky. The repairman, after checking the lines, valves, and connections, may discover that the pilot jet simply needs to be re-lit. You pay him for his house call and wonder why you didn't check the damn pilot (assuming you could find it) before you called him. Or you may turn out to be unlucky, which is invariably the case. You are told to prepare to welcome a new water tank into the house. You calculate the costs to the accompaniment of more and even choicer basement blasphemy.

You receive explicit instructions on how to locate and light the pilot jet. You file away the guarantee and prepare yourself for other problems, but the whole incident has subtly reminded you how important water is to the life of man—not merely hot water for a necessary shower but water per se. Shutting off the water at the main valve means no drinking, no washing of hands, no flushing, etc. You remember reading somewhere that forty-eight hours without water is a death sentence for a human being (with some exceptions, of course). All this bring you back to a simple strategic law—control their water, and you can control a population, a people, the whole human race, which is 96 percent water to begin with.

The failings of appliances do not have the impact of water tank deaths, by any means. These are more than annoyances but less than total stoppages. The bearings in the washing machine or dryer may start to grind before giving out completely, but this might mean a mere delay in doing the laundry for a day or so. A fuse may blow out. A circuit may "short." These are minor in comparison to major setbacks.

I have learned that the most major of all setbacks is related to plumbing. Electrical failures are a close second (there are candles to provide some light, after all). But when the drains clog or when the sewer backs up or when the commodes develop sluggish flushes or when the tubs won't drain at all, then the problems are mortal—fixable but mortal. Until or unless they are fixed, normal domestic life cannot go on. And in almost all such cases the house-owner is at the total mercy of the plumber.

I've thought lately how much social and political power resides in the hands of plumbers. Should they develop the national or international unity that would permit them to act in concert, their power would be formidable and irresistible. Should they decide as a unit not to fix commodes or remedy other forms of house constipation, they could bring societies to a standstill. (In larger terms they might even be capable of settling matters of war and peace.) By creating such ruptures or cloggings, the slow thief plays right into the hands of plumbers who, like doctors or dentists, await the inevitable.

Because plumbers note details of which amateurs take no notice at all, they have a lingo all their own. Once, after installing a new commode in a downstairs auxiliary bathroom, one plumber of happy memory surveyed his work, smiled at me, and said, as if he were reciting a poem, "It has a nice, soft flush, doesn't it?" On another occasion, dealing with a different plumber who was reaming an outside sewer line and bringing up buckets of muck and other sludge and filth, I asked him how he could do this kind of work and not get sick to his stomach. He looked at me in casual disbelief and said, "You're really not a plumber unless you can do this and eat a sandwich at the same time."

Another aspect of domestic life at which the slow thief excels, albeit through his denizens, is the continual creation of waste. As the owner of a house in a Pittsburgh suburb where garbage is collected once a week, I am always impressed by how much waste a modest house of six rooms can create. The result is that every Wednesday night I lug to the corner of my lot black plastic bags crammed with everything from used paper towels to crushed boxes, milk cartons, and ungrindable steak bones. Also, I've become quite conscientious about separately packing recyclables such as glass jars and plastic liters. I realize the necessity of this in patriotic terms, but simultaneously I can't rid myself of the knowledge that I'm doing the basic labor for the benefit and profit of the recyclers who will take what I've cleaned and gathered and then convert it into what can be used again.

One occasionally annoying habit of all slow thieves is their proclivity to keep all those outside of the house outside. In other words, houses do not take kindly to being entered by anyone other than their rightful owners, and this is at face value commendable. But a problem arises when owners of houses forget or lose their keys, making themselves hostage to lockouts of their own creation. This is a true crisis, particularly when the owner has spent a great deal on security and other protective devices. So resourceful are some owners that they, when confronted by an unexpected lockout, have to resort to extreme measures to gain access once more to their own property. A house is not an automobile, after all, whose locked doors can be jimmied open with comparative ease by the car thief in each of us. But being confronted by double locks, deadbolts, burglar-alarm systems, and canines is not just a change in degree but in kind in the ongoing war between house-owners and the outside world.

Once, when my son was fourteen months old, my mother-in-law accidentally locked herself out of the house, leaving my son alone and making her desperate. Within half an hour my mother-in-law, my wife, several neighbors, two policemen, and several firemen (complete with fire truck) were on the scene. My son, I was told, was watching this gathering from the living-room window. He was laughing, waving, and applauding. Meanwhile, the firemen were conferring with my wife to determine which window she would prefer them to break in order to gain entry. Finally, one of the policemen asked if anyone had asked my son to open the front door. The answer was no. The policeman then walked to the living-room window and said, "Hey, kid, open the front door." A minute later my son did as he was told, and the crisis ended. But what is important to note here is that salvation came from within, not from without. From without, the fireman's request to break a window was certainly sensible. Such an entry would have been tantamount to a break-in, but there seemed to be no alternative. People in such circumstances, unless they have hidden a spare key under the Welcome mat or given one to a neighbor for "emergency" use, become hostages to their own security measures. And their failure to gain entry often proves to them how effective these security measures actually are. Thus, owners who are locked out are placed in a position of having to think like thieves in order to break into their own houses. So, ironically, it's a thief against the slow thief, as if one has the need to create the other.

This business of replacing, updating, or simply remodeling is essential to every house-owner's spirit of personal renewal, which is a garden in perpetual need of watering. Like cities, houses are always, in large or small ways, under construction. Every house-owner's deepest wish is that the improvements and replacements and renewals will end and that the house will simply be, a thing existing in time but spared time's ravages. But the existentialist in him acknowledges that this is impossible. So, like Sisyphus, he begins to push the rock of renewal up Time's mountain, and that in effect becomes the basic rhythm of his life. There is a certain tiredness in it, to be sure. There is a certain repetitiveness in it as well. But there is also a satisfaction in it that can only be known by the renewer in the very act of renewing.

Houses, of course, eventually take on the personalities of those who live in them, and this gives them a kind of sanctity. We have all had the experience of visiting what I call "designers' houses," which bear the mark of the architects and interior designers who have created them but reveal little if anything of the character of their live-in owners. The sterility is palpable. But a lived-in house is like a favorite sweater. It fits. We wear it, and not it, us. It reflects our taste and our preference. We're at home with it.

This is especially true when a house is not just a domicile but a place of work. The lives of many writers attest to this. Hemingway's *finca* is now a shrine in Cuba, and the managers of the estate have made sure that his newspapers, books, and the stand-up desk where he did his writing-typing are preserved exactly as he left them, as if he has gone out temporarily and will shortly return. The *finca* was Hemingway's workshop; his mark was on it.

The same holds true of the sidehouses in Massachusetts where Archibald MacLeish wrote his poems and plays in Conway, and where Richard Wilbur crafts his Mozartian poems and translations in Cummington. But nowhere is this marriage of writer and shelter more evident than in Robinson Jeffers's Tor House along the northern California coast. Jeffers built the house, stone by stone, refusing all help from outsiders even when it was given in good faith. For Jeffers, the matter of owning a house was similar to William Morris's concept of authorship. For Morris, an author could not call a book his own unless he had written it, designed it, manufactured the paper (and, presumably, the ink as well), bound it, and stamped the spine and front cover. Then and only then could the author say it was his book. Jeffers's building of Tor House reflected this same purity and totality of authorship. He designed it, not only on paper but also as he worked. He lugged stones and boulders from the Pacific shore to the building site, lifted or levered them into position, crafted the furnishings when he had completed the job, and, like Yeats in Ballylee, lived there with his family.

You really have to visit Tor House to feel what I mean here. Surrounded now by other houses so that it's integrated into an upper-middle-class California coastal neighborhood, Tor House still testifies to the individuality of the man who made it. After you tour the rooms, climb the modest tower that Jeffers built for his wife and marvel at how one man inexperienced in house architecture somehow managed to create so symmetrical and distinctive a place against the Pacific winds; you stand back and simply appreciate the sheer impudence of the effort. Later you think of Jeffers dying in the first-floor bedroom of Tor House, and his death blesses the place like a silent amen. To build with one's own hands a house of stone, to write your poems and plays in it, to raise your family in it, and then in the fullness of time to take your last breath in it seems like a complete and completed circle. It quietly proclaims that this is how men's lives should evolve and end—in familiar, lived-in surroundings. This is one thing that the slow thief cannot steal. Why? Because his very slowness and thievery have had a hand in creating it from the very beginning.

When it comes to knowing in advance that you have only a finite time to live, what better place is there to face the inevitable than in one's most familiar surroundings? It certainly seems to me preferable to ending in a hospice or a hospital room. How many times have I heard those dying in a room other than their own (heard it in fact or from others who had heard it in fact) say, "I never thought it would end this way." It was not only their condition but the strangeness of their surroundings that probably prompted such a remark.

Having mentioned writers, I'm suddenly reminded of the relation of literature to domestic life. In my experience I've noticed that truly good writing (with certain exceptions, of course) is rarely done on the run or even on the road. Journalism may happen this way, but literature (or what comes in time to be regarded as literature) needs more gestation. Writers usually rely on a period of withdrawal from a particular experience before they feel qualified or inspired to write about it (to represent it in language, that is, to repeat what was once present, to re-present it, in words that re-create it). This may not happen for years. But when it does, it frequently happens in domestic surroundings or the equivalent. The magnetism of home cannot be underestimated as a place where a writer's thoughts and feelings are gradually distilled into the wine of a vision. And when such circumstances do not exist in fact for one reason or another, writers often create their facsimiles. It is not uncommon for their very subject matter to reflect this. After James Joyce left Ireland, to which he returned only once in his life thereafter, he wrote in Trieste, Paris, and other locations, but Ireland—Dublin, particularly—remained his subject for the rest of his life. Hemingway wrote many of his Michigan stories in France. And I could make a similar claim for some of the work of F. Scott Fitzgerald, e. e. cummings, and Hart Crane.

I will even go a step further and state that the subject of the most enduring works of literature—tragedies and comedies—is domestic. Travel writing, reportage, and even epics such as the *Iliad* and T. E. Lawrence's *Seven Pillars of Wisdom* may be powerful in their subject matter, but we often find ourselves reading them as spectators. We share the sense of adventure, but it is not an intimate experience. When the subject matter is domestic, we immediately identify with the characters and circumstances. Why? Because our familiarity with domestic life leaves us sensitive to the whole chromatic scale of possibilities. Whether they have actually happened to us is irrelevant. We know they could happen, and our imaginations take over from there. Take any of the Greek tragedies or comedies, for example. In one way or another the drama arises from some domestic conflict. The result may be tragic, as it is in *Oedipus, Antigone,* and *Medea,* or it may be comic, as Aristophanes demonstrated in *Lysistrata.* The same is true of the comedies and tragedies of Shakespeare. They are all rooted in domestic situations. This is true even of *Julius Caesar,* if one considers the scene between Caesar and Calpurnia, as well as the scene between Brutus and Portia, essential to the tragedy of both men. And essential they are. In summary, the tragic and comic threads in Greek and Shakespearian plays are rooted in what we all recognize as domestic, and the word itself (as we must occasionally remind ourselves) is derived from *domus,* the Latin word for house.

Human life begins in wombs, but our lives thereafter evolve in rooms. And in due course they frequently end there. Churchill referred to his country house, Chartwell, as his "habitation," and he returned there periodically during his public life before he lodged there permanently in his final years. Similarly, Charles de Gaulle withdrew to his home village of Colombey-les-deux-Eglises at the end of his life. Harry Truman went back to Independence, Missouri; and Dwight Eisenhower, a soldier with many addresses, drew strength from his adopted home in Gettysburg, Pennsylvania, and died there. Some primordial tug summoned them all back, as it does or as it will all of us, in spirit if not in fact. No matter when it does, the slow thief will be waiting there to welcome us.

Chapter 1. Poetry and Public Speech

Saint Paul's phrases appear in 1 Corinthians 13:1.

Robert Frost's letter to Sidney Cox (December 1914) is from *Frost: Collected Poems, Prose and Plays* (Library of America, 1995), 681. All subsequent references to and quotes from Frost are from this volume.

The full quote from Thoreau is "For it matters not how small the beginning may seem to be, what is once well done is done forever." It can be found in his essay on "Civil Disobedience," *The Writings of Henry David Thoreau*, vol. 4 (Houghton Mifflin, 1906), 370.

I. F. Stone's "all governments lie" appears explicitly or in only slightly different words in many of his columns and books. It became so identified with him that Myra MacPherson titled her award-winning biography of Stone *All Governments Lie* (Simon & Schuster, 2009).

Robert Desnos's curse appears under the title of "Dove in the Arch" in *The Voice* (Grossman, 1972).

The quote from Hayden Carruth is actually the title of his anthology of contemporary American poetry.

T. S. Eliot is quoted from his *Selected Prose*, edited by Frank Kermode (Harcourt Brace Jovanovich, 1975).

In Shakespeare's *Hamlet,* Act III, "flesh is heir to" is part of Hamlet's best-known soliloquy.

Richard Wilbur's phrase is from his essay "Poetry and Happiness," included in *Responses: Prose Pieces, 1953–1976* (Harcourt Brace Jovanovich, 1976).

Ezra Pound is quoted from "The Constant Preaching to the Mob," *Literary Essays* (New Directions, 1935).

The poem from which the image by George Seferis is taken is "Mathios Pascalis Among the Roses," *Collected Poems* (Princeton University Press, 1995).

The famous lines of Antonio Machado are from "Proverbs and Song Verse," in *Antonio Machado: Selected Poems,* translated by Alan Trueblood (Harvard University Press, 1982).

John Donne's "The Paradox" is from *Poems of John Donne,* edited by H. Grierson (Oxford University Press, 1963).

The passage from Edmond Rostand's *Cyrano de Bergerac* is from Christopher Fry's translation (Oxford University Press, 1975).

The quote from Saint-John Perse is the last sentence of his introduction to his *Collected Poems* (Princeton University Press, 1995).

Chapter 2. Power and Pretense

The quote from Paul Valéry is from his *Reflections on the World Today* (Pantheon, 1948), 28.

Charles Lindbergh's description of this incident appears in *Of Flight and Life* (Scribner's, 1948).

Ezra Pound's translation of "The Seafarer" was first published in *Ripostes* (Ovid Press, 1911). It has been reprinted and anthologized many times.

The importance of Abraham Lincoln's stepmother, Sarah Johnston, to his life appears in every biography of Lincoln but is, in my opinion, understated. I prefer my interpretation.

Jon Meacham's concept of power appears in "The Story of Power," which ran in the December 20, 2008, issue of *Newsweek*.

The references to Cocteau and Om Khalsoum are gleaned from newspaper accounts that I read at the time as well as from my conversations with various people during trips to Paris and one trip to Cairo.

Chapter 3. Strike Down the Band

The Shakespearian lines are from *The Merchant of Venice*, Act V.

The statement by David Alfaro Siqueiros appears below one of his murals in the art museum in Mexico City.

The comment from A. Whitney Griswold is from *Liberal Education and the Democratic Ideal* (Yale University Press, 1950).

The military costs are those released by the Department of Defense after the turn of the century, and the art expenditures per citizen for the countries mentioned are from the same time period. Although the actual figures would be larger now, I suspect that the percentages would be the same. David McCullough's comment was made following an address he delivered in Pittsburgh, Pennsylvania.

The comment by John Ciardi was made at the conclusion of a poetry reading in Pittsburgh, Pennsylvania, a few months before his death.

Chapter 4. The Lasting Marriage of Knowledge and Belief

All the references to John Henry Cardinal Newman are from *The Scope and Nature of University Education* (J. M. Dent, 1956).

Quotations of T. S. Eliot are from *Essays Ancient and Modern* (Harcourt, Brace and World, 1932).

The lines from John Donne's "Satire, III" are found in the Grierson edition previously cited (chapter 1).

What is relevant about the Hutchins reference is the title of his talk.

Chapter 5. Belief and the Critic

My quotations from literary critics and references to their critical views are drawn from my reading of the following works: M. H. Abrams, *Literature and Belief* (Columbia University Press, 1958); Kenneth Clark, *The Nude* (Doubleday, 1959); H. Coombes, *Literature and Criticism* (Chatto & Windus, 1953); David Daiches, *A Study of Literature for Readers and Critics* (Cornell University Press, 1948) and *Poetry and the Modern World* (University of Chicago Press, 1940); C. Day Lewis, *The Lyric Impulse* (Harvard University Press, 1965); T. S. Eliot, *The Sacred Wood* (Methuen, 1920) and *Selected Essays* (Harcourt Brace, 1968); Helen Gardner, *Religion and Literature* (Oxford University Press, 1971); Richard Horchler, "Literature and Morality," *Commonweal* 69 (1959); James Craig La Drière, *Directions in Contemporary Criticism and Literary Scholarship* (Bruce, 1953); Jacques Maritain, *Art and Scholasticism* (Scribner's, 1920) and *Creative Intuition in Art and Poetry* (Princeton University Press, 1953); Walter Ong, S.J., "The Jinnee in the Well Wrought Urn," *The Barbarian Within, and Other Fugitive Essays and Studies* (Macmillan, 1962); Herbert Read, *The Nature of Literature* (Horizon Press, 1956); William J. Rooney, *The Problem of "Poetry and Belief" in Contemporary Criticism* (Catholic University of America Press, 1949); Nathan A. Scott, ed., *The New Orpheus* (Sheed & Ward, 1964) (essays by W. K. Wimsatt, T. S. Eliot, Charles Moeller, and Scott himself are among the essays anthologized here); Martin Turnell, *Poetry and Crisis* (Paladin, 1938) and *Modern Literature and Christian Faith* (Newman, 1961); and Eliseo Vivas, *The Problems of Aesthetics* (Holt, Rinehart and Winston, 1953).

Briefer references are made to the following: Edmund Blunden, *Wilfred Owen, Poems* (1949); Babette Deutsch, *Poetry in Our Time* (Holt, 1952); Maurice DeWulf, *Art and Beauty* (Herder, 1950); Leslie Fiedler, *Toward an Amateur Criticism* (1950); Harold J. Gardiner, S.J., *Norms for the Novel* (America Press, 1953); Charles Moeller, *Freedom and Truth* (1954); Thomas Pollock, *The Nature of Literature* (Princeton University Press, 1942); John Press, *The Chequer'd Shade: Reflections on Obscurity in Poetry* (Oxford University Press, 1958); Philip Scharper, *The Natural Novel: An Appraisal* (1956); Nathan A. Scott, *The Collaboration of Vision in the Poetic*

Act: The Religious Dimension (1958); and Dylan Thomas, *Quite Early One Morning* (New Directions, 1954).

Quotations from the poems of Wilfred Owen are from *Wilfred Owen: The Complete Poems and Fragments,* edited by Jon Stallworthy (Norton, 1983).

Chapter 6. Endthoughts of a Recent Retiree

The Giamatti reference is to his *A Free and Ordered Space* (Norton, 1976), and the comment by Hutchins is from Milton Mayer's *Robert Maynard Hutchins: A Memoir* (University of California Press, 1983).

The quote of More is from William Roper's famous *The Life of Sir Thomas More.*

Chapter 7. Provence of the Six Winds

I was originally contracted to write this essay by an editor of the *National Geographic Magazine.* It was never published because the editor resigned while I was in France and was succeeded by one who preferred to publish only those writers whom he himself contracted. Much that is in the essay is derived from what one can only learn through travel, and the rest deals directly with the culture and history of the South of France. For the latter I steeped myself in books by the shelf, but my final indebtednesses were to the following: on troubadour verse generally, *Proensa: An Anthology of Troubadour Poetry,* selected and translated by Paul Blackburn, edited with an introduction by George Economou (University of California Press, 1978); L. J. B. Bérenger Féraud, *Les Provençaux à travers les âges* (E. Leroux, 1900); Roderick Cameron, *The Golden Riviera* (Weidenfeld & Nicolson, 1975); Denis de Rougemont, *Love in the Western World* (Pantheon, 1940); Ford Madox Ford, *Provence* (Lippincott, 1935); Michael Jacobs, *Provence* (Viking, 1988) (including the quote from Victor Hugo); Bo Niles, *A Window on Provence* (Penguin, 1991); James Pope-Hennessy, *Aspects of Provence* (Penguin, 1988); Laura Raison, *The South of France* (Beaufort, 1985). Other books that were helpful or from which I quoted passages or sentences were *Poems of René Char*, translated by Mary Ann Caws and Jonathan Griffin (Princeton, 1976); Giovanna Magi, *Provence* (Bonechi, 1984, English ed.); Stendahl, *Travels in the South of France* (Orion, 1970); and Georges Ramié's tribute to Picasso in *Ceramics of Picasso* (Ediciones Poligrafa, 1985). A great deal was derived from what I heard or saw en route.

Chapter 8. Why Go Anywhere Whenever?

Crucial in my writing of this essay was Alastair Reid's *Whereabouts* (North Point, 1987). I have quoted Czeslaw Milosz from conversation during one of his visits to Pittsburgh for the International Poetry Forum. I have also quoted from Marianne Moore's poem "Poetry" and from Philip Booth's "Letter from a Distant Land."

Chapter 9. Remembering Gregory Peck

Almost everything in this essay is a result of the personal contact or conversations I had with Gregory Peck during the last years of his life. I did consult several books about his films, the most helpful of them being Lynn Haney's *Gregory Peck: A Charmed Life* (Carroll & Graf, 2003).

Chapter 10. To Wrestle a Slow Thief

The anecdotes about the return of Churchill, de Gaulle, Truman, and Eisenhower to their homes of choice are now a matter of public knowledge.

The author of more than thirty books of poetry, fiction, essays, and plays, Samuel Hazo is the founder and director of the International Poetry Forum in Pittsburgh, Pennsylvania. He is also McAnulty Distinguished Professor of English Emeritus at Duquesne University. From 1950 to 1957 he served in the United States Marine Corps, completing his tour as a captain. He was graduated magna cum laude from the University of Notre Dame and received his master's degree from Duquesne University and his doctorate from the University of Pittsburgh. Some of his most recent books are *Like a Man Gone Mad* and *The Song of the Horse* (poetry), *This Part of the World* (fiction), *The Power of Less* (essays), and *Watching Fire, Watching Rain* (drama). He has also translated essays by Denis de Rougemont and the poems of Adonis and Nadia Tueni. His book of poems, *Just Once: New and Previous Poems,* won the Maurice English Poetry Award in 2003. The University of Notre Dame, from which he received the Griffin Award for Creative Writing in 2005, conferred the tenth of his eleven honorary doctorates in 2008. A National Book Award finalist, he was chosen the first State Poet of the Commonwealth of Pennsylvania by Governor Robert Casey in 1993, and he served in that post until 2003.